Mindset *Matters*

A Curriculum to Help Students
Understand how to Help Themselves Succeed
with a **GROWTH MINDSET**

NATIONAL CENTER for
YOUTH ISSUES

P.O. Box 22185 • Chattanooga, TN 37422-2185
423-899-5714 • 866-318-6294
fax: 423-899-4547 • www.ncyi.org

NATIONAL CENTER for
YOUTH ISSUES

P.O. Box 22185
Chattanooga, TN 37422-2185
423-899-5714 • 866-318-6294
fax: 423-899-4547
www.ncyi.org

ISBN: 978-1-937870-40-9 $27.95
© 2016 National Center for Youth Issues, Chattanooga, TN
All rights reserved.

Written by: Lisa King, Ed.S, LPC
Contributing Editor: Beth Spencer Rabon
Design: Phillip Rodgers
Published by National Center for Youth Issues

Printed at Starkey Printing, Chattanooga, Tennessee, U.S.A., July 2018

TABLE OF CONTENTS

Chapter 5: **Self-Talk**

Chapter 6: **Everyone is Unique**

Chapter 7: **Teach Others What You Know**

PART THREE: APPENDIX

Mindset Matters

Part **ONE** 1

INTRODUCTION

How this Curriculum Came to Be...

As a school counselor in an elementary school, I am always looking for a fresh approach to teach "how to do your best." When I learned about Carol Dweck's body of research on Growth Mindset, I was excited to see that she had found positive outcomes in student achievement in teaching this theory to students. I was excited and interested in finding out more. It was on my to-do list, my "maybe I'll integrate that into my curriculum someday" list. Then, on a plane ride home this past summer, I browsed my on-board movie list to find that Carol Dweck's TED talk was available. Game changer. Yes, this 10 minute video turned my to-do list desire into action.

To understand the subsequent pages and the ideas within this book, allow me to present the overview of this Curriculum with a Top 5 reasons I think it works (in no particular order):

1. **FLEXIBILITY:** At first I thought about creating a small group curriculum surrounding this idea, but as I did more research, I wanted to make this curriculum accessible for both small group and classroom curriculum. I wanted to create a curriculum that is easy to use, easy to get buy-in from teachers and students and that is FLEXIBLE. I use a certain curriculum in kindergarten (*Peaceworks I-Care Rules*) because I can teach those 5 rules in any way I want. However, *I Care Cat* and his 5 *I-Care Rules* give me a framework and room to be creative within that framework.

2. **RESEARCH-BASED:** Google one of these: "Growth Mindset," "Carol Dweck." Prepare to have your mind blown. There are some smart people involved in these studies. As you see from the table below (*Mindsets in the Classroom* by Mary Cay Ricci © 2013, Prufrock Press, pg. 11,) children start off their elementary school career having a growth mindset. They think that they can do anything! But as they get older, they start thinking about how things are harder. They form more of a fixed mindset, as the culture of our society trains them in a way to quash their optimism and lends them to a more fixed mindset of searching for praise instead of progress. This curriculum is great for elementary age children so that we can teach growth mindset at a young age.

Table 1
Changes in Fixed and Growth Mindsets Across Grade Levels

Grade	Fixed Mindset	Growth Mindset
K	n/a	100%
1	10%	90%
2	18%	82%
3	42%	58%

3. **KIDS LIKE IT:** I have had a student write me an individual referral form to learn more about the brain (really!). I have parent emails telling me how their son is coming home talking about our Mindset group. When kids have fun and find interest in a topic, they want to talk about it. That is just cool.

4. **CONNECTS WITH ACADEMICS:** When you are talking to students about grit, stamina, how to get smarter and get better outcomes, teachers like it. Academic connections are essential for counselors to make. It's one of the ASCA domains because it is critical for us to teach at the elementary level.

5. **STRUCTURE FOR YOUR YEAR:** One of the things that threads through these lessons is what I call the Mindset Chant (page 13). This chant talks about "Training your Brain," and that can be tied into any skill-based lesson we do. Make this curriculum a universal theme for a grade level worth of lessons or to integrate if you are a Mindset School.

More about the Structure (a/k/a Making it Easy to Follow)

For either small group or classroom lessons, having a structured curriculum is easy for students to follow and easy for us to implement. Aligned with each letter of the word **MINDSET**, this curriculum has 6 learning topics: **M**indfulness, **I**dentify Brain Basics, **N**ot Yet is OK (a/k/a the Power of Yet), **D**etermination and Grit, **S**elf-Talk, **E**veryone is Unique, and the last letter T is for **T**eaching Others (because we know that when students show mastery, then they can teach others what they have learned.)

As you can see in more detail on page 33, Mindset Matters can be taught in as few or as many sessions as desired. The recurring theme of this curriculum is training and understanding your brain so that you can show the world you can get smarter with effort. Many major teaching points are reflected in the Mindset Chant (page 13) which reinforces the essence of the Growth Mindset theory, so you will see it in many of the lessons within the curriculum. Also, because most counselors like to adapt their lessons to their time frames and comfort levels, this curriculum gives a framework of the topics and allows counselors some latitude. For example, if you have a lesson on determination, you can use that in lieu of the ideas provided here. It's up to you!

Tell me more about the background of this... what IS growth mindset??

> "In a fixed mindset students believe their basic abilities, their intelligence, their talents, are just fixed traits. They have a certain amount and that's that, and then their goal becomes to look smart all the time and never look dumb. In a growth mindset students understand that their talents and abilities can be developed through effort, good teaching and persistence. They don't necessarily think everyone's the same or anyone can be Einstein, but they believe everyone can get smarter if they work at it."

The above quote describes Fixed vs. Growth Mindset. It is about teaching kids that with effort they can get smarter and grow their brains. Research tells us that kids who learn about Growth Mindset actually **DO BETTER**. Growth mindset promotes that one's ability can be developed through dedication and hard work; brains and innate talent are just the starting point.

Many of us work with students who believe that they will not amount to much, kids who realize that they are in remedial classes or in a cycle of poverty. To teach them (and watch them get) that they create their future is awesome. And thank you to Dr. Dweck and the many scientists and psychologists that have done the work that has provided the opportunity to create ideas surrounding a research-based theory.

Why No Discussion of Fixed Mindset

As I read Carol Dweck's book, *Mindset: The New Psychology of Success (2007),* I was excited to create lessons about this great theory. I jumped into a third grade class the following week and did a lesson on Growth Mindset vs. Fixed Mindset. It was not a success. The students at the elementary level seemed confused by which one was which. I actually stopped teaching about Growth Mindset for about a year, until the idea of breaking Growth Mindset down into skills occurred to me. SO, teaching what Growth Mindset IS rather than what it ISN'T has proven much more successful. Focusing on what has been successful is what growth mindset is about, hence this curriculum has not spent much time on defining or learning about Fixed Mindset.

Download the PowerPoint file to guide you through this lesson at: **www.ncyi.org/ mindsetmatters**	**PPTS to Guide You** If you see this icon, this means the lesson you are reading about has a PowerPoint to guide your lesson. Why recreate the wheel? Use this as a guide for your students and also for you.

Create a Growth Mindset Culture

Ideas to create a Growth Mindset culture in your school are:

- Make Growth Mindset your school-wide theme.

- Have staff book studies.

- Have student small counseling groups using this curriculum.

- Use this curriculum for core lessons in the classroom.

- Show video clips listed on page 163 at staff meetings.

- Encourage teachers to create brain stations in their classroom and ask counselors to have one in their office.

Create Brain Stations

Brain Stations are corners or nooks in a classroom or office with gadgets, books, and fidgets about brains. Why? This is a great place where kids can explore and remember that their brain can be trained. Brains can grow with the practice of skills. Some classes have cool down corners, so why not add this to your room, too? Encourage kids to realize that they are in control of how smart they can be.

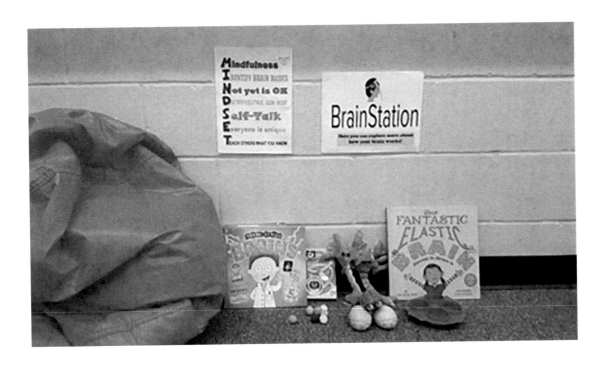

BrainStation

Here you can explore more about how your brain works!

What's the "Mindset Chant"?

Kids remember songs and chants. This one has motions. Even better, right? I made this up, taught the students, and it stuck. It embodies what we are trying to teach about Growth Mindset. It can be done in class, group, on morning announcements, made into a video, etc.

Leader: Whatcha gotta do?

Class: I've got to train my brain.

(Motion: Make a muscle and then point to brain.)

Leader: Why you gotta do it?

Class: Gotta show the world.

(Motion: Hand over eyes, like you are searching)

Leader: Whatcha gonna show them?

Class: That I've got some skills.

(Motion: Point to yourself with both thumbs)

Leader: What kind of skills?

Class: Whatever I work on!

(Motion: Wag pointer finger at someone and say in a silly voice)

Leader: What's that called?

Class: Growth Mindset, Growth Mindset, Growth Mindset

(Motion: Do a little dance)

See the next page for a mini poster of the chant that can be printed out for classrooms. It is also available for download (p13_Mindset Chant.pdf) so you can display it in a PowerPoint presentation, Smartboard, etc.

Download and print the reproducible pdf at:
www.ncyi.org/ mindsetmatters

MINDSET CHANT!

Whatcha gotta do?

I've got to train my brain.

Why you gotta do it?

Gotta show the world.

Whatcha gonna show them?

That I've got some skills.

What kind of skills?

Whatever I work on!

What's that called?

Growth Mindset, Growth Mindset,
Growth Mindset!

Let's do the
MINDSET CHANT

Leader: Whatcha gotta do?

Class: **I've got to train my brain.**

Leader: Why you gotta do it?

Class: **Gotta show the world.**

Leader: Whatcha gonna show them?

Class: **That I've got some skills.**

Leader: What kind of skills?

Class: **Whatever I work on!**

Leader: What's that called?

Class: **Growth Mindset,
Growth Mindset, Growth Mindset!**

Coloring Sheets to Help Reinforce the Curriculum Structure

The lessons in this curriculum are set up by each letter in the word Mindset. On the following pages are some mini posters to help promote these ideas on bulletin boards, wall displays, or class/group coloring activities for reinforcing the concepts.

First, on page 16, you will see a mini poster of all the letters/topics on one page.

- This can be used as a coloring sheet or a guide for your lessons. You can color (or have students color) the letter that you are teaching in that session.

- This can be hung in classrooms as a reminder of what was taught in lessons.

Next, on pages 17-23, there are mini posters with each letter on a separate page. These can be used as follows:

- On bulletin boards

- To have each member of the class/group take one letter and decorate it, writing what was learned in this topic

- To have students color in as you progressively get to that topic

Mindfulness

IDENTIFY BRAIN BASICS

Not yet is OK

DETERMINATION AND GRIT

Self-Talk

Everyone is unique

TEACH OTHERS WHAT YOU KNOW

INDFULNESS

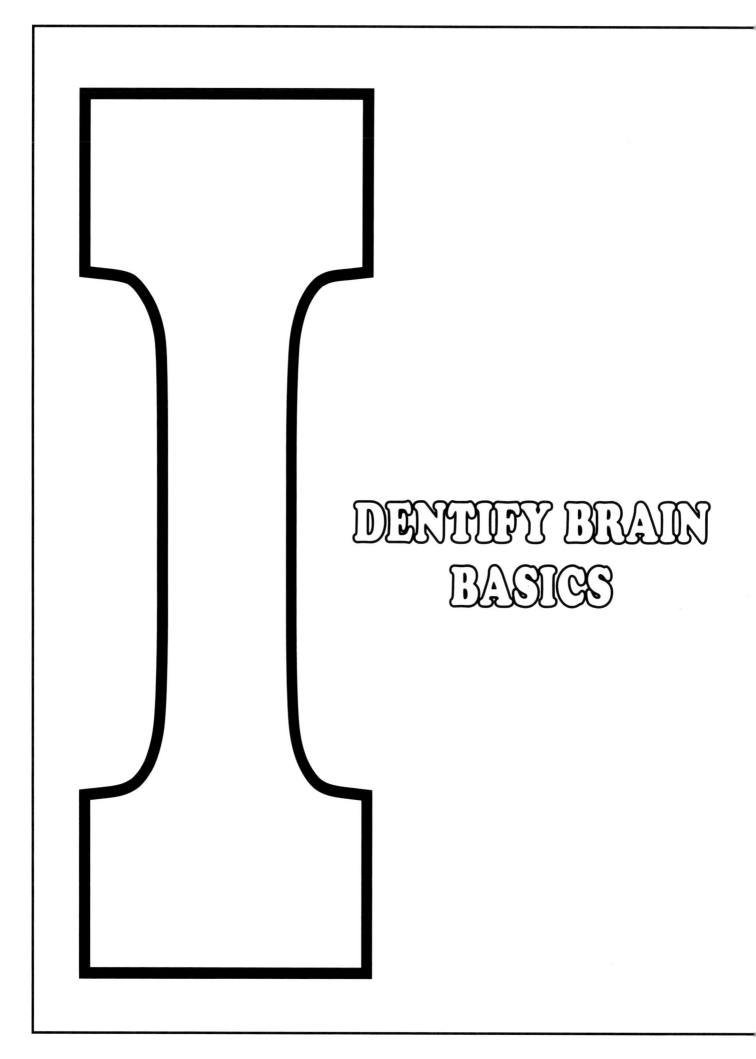

IDENTIFY BRAIN BASICS

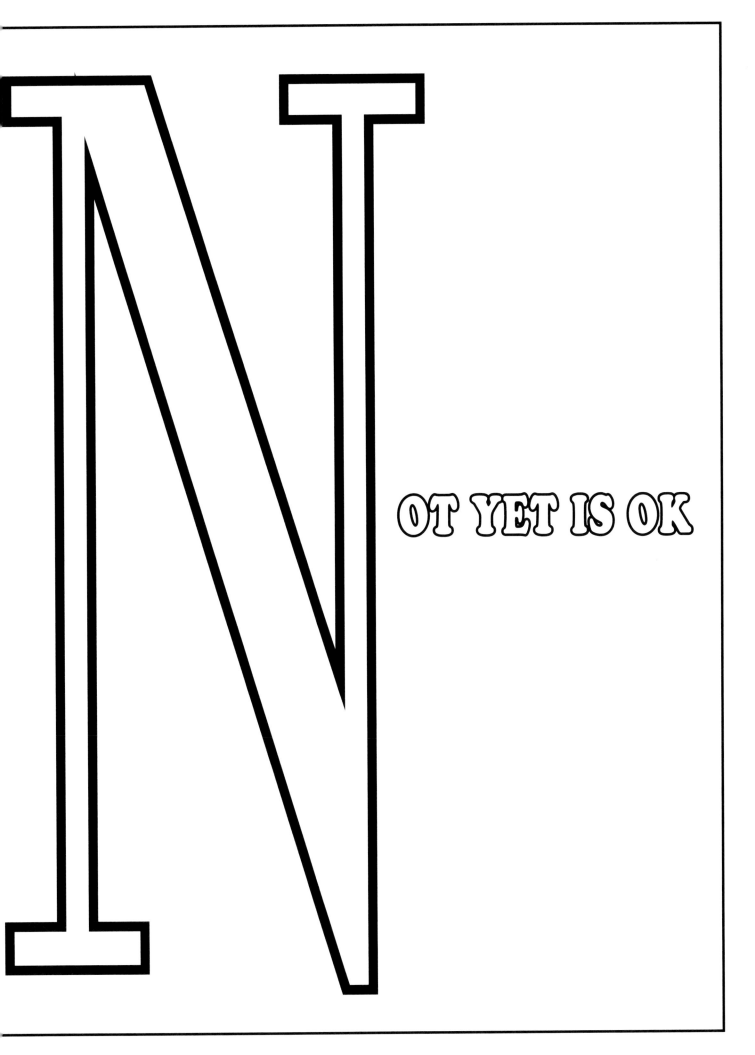

N

OT YET IS OK

ETERMINATION
AND GRIT

ELF-TALK

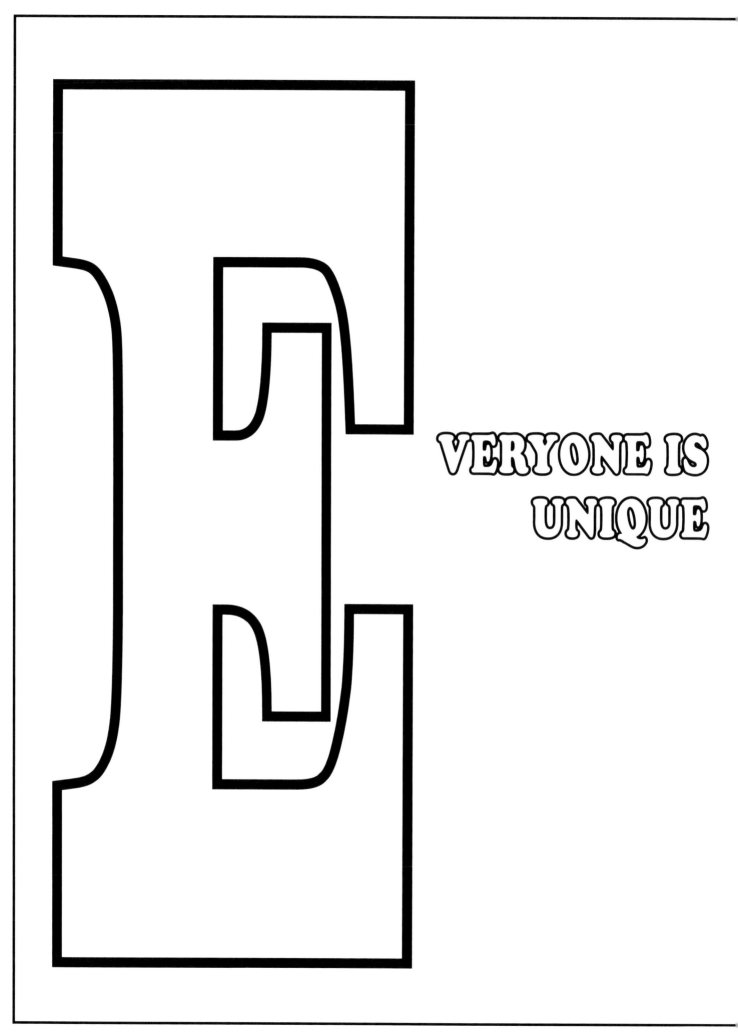

VERYONE IS
UNIQUE

EACH OTHERS WHAT YOU KNOW

Mindset Matters for Small Group Counseling

In the next few pages you will find forms that will help in creating a Mindset Matters small group. You will find:

I. Small Group Counseling Sample Email to Teachers

II. Group Outline Template

III. Group Outline Template Sample

IV. Mindset Matters Group Permission Slip

V. Teacher/Parent Pre-Post Survey

VI. Student Pre-Post Survey (Grades 4-6)

VII. Student Pre-Post Survey (Grades 2-4)

VIII. Group Reminder Cards

No matter what your ability is, effort is what ignites that ability and turns it into accomplishment.

– Carol S. Dweck
Mindset: The New Psychology Of Success

In the fixed mindset, when you fail; you're a failure– In the growth moindset, when you fail; you're learning.

Small Group Counseling Sample Email to Teachers

Teachers,

I would like to invite students to participate in a small group counseling experience and would love for you to email referrals to me. The curriculum I will follow is called "Mindset Matters," and the goal of this group will be to help students realize that they control their future. We will work on concepts such as positive self-talk, determination/grit, and understanding that we all have different paces of learning (a/k/a It's alright it you don't get it YET).

The concepts in this curriculum are part of a growing body of research regarding GROWTH MINDSET. I feel pretty passionate about what I have been learning and look forward to presenting it as part of the curriculum. I will introduce this to your whole classes during our lessons as well. Please take 10 minutes to watch this TED talk by Carol Dweck, a Stanford University professor who has found that when kids are taught a growth mindset, their achievement scores, grades, and self-concept go up. (She has done the research in low income schools and proven it... how cool!!)

Carol Dweck's TED Talk
https://www.ted.com/speakers/carol_dweck

Thanks for your support!

Your school counselor

Group Outline Template

NAME	TEACHER	PERMISSION	1	2	3	4	5	6	7	8

	ACTIVITY	MATERIALS
SESSION 1 DATE_____		
SESSION 2 DATE_____		
SESSION 3 DATE_____		
SESSION 4 DATE_____		
SESSION 5 DATE_____		
SESSION 6 DATE_____		
SESSION 7 DATE_____		
SESSION 8 DATE_____		
SESSION 9 DATE_____		

Group Outline Template Sample

NAME	TEACHER	PERMISSION	1	2	3	4	5	6	7	8
Naya	Julian	X								
Vera	Julian	X								
Ethan	Resudek	X								
Aiydan	Resudek	X								
Tarik	Tyson	X								
Bryan	Tyson	X								
Cara	Barker	X								

	ACTIVITY	MATERIALS
SESSION 1 DATE 9/16	Introductions. Review Group Rules Do an Icebreaker Have students complete Pre Group Survey	See pre-post survey page 29.
SESSION 2 DATE 10/7	**MINDFULNESS** Watch video and do lesson that goes along with creating Mindful Minute Bottles	See pages 55-56. Water bottles empty, clear glue, glitter, food coloring
SESSION 3 DATE 10/14	Continue decorating Mindful Minute Bottles	See pages 55-56. Send home letter to parents on page 57.
SESSION 4 DATE 10/21	**IDENTIFY BRAIN BASICS** Teach students the Mindset Chant Begin talking about Brain Basics	Watch Video: Ned the Neuron.
SESSION 5 DATE 10/28	Brain Connections A Yummy Lesson	Lesson on pages 68-69. Peel and Pull Licorice
SESSION 6 DATE 11/2	**NOT YET AND DETERMINATION** Game Day	Download "MSM_PowerPoint 4" from website (www.ncyi.org/mindsetmatters). Lesson page 100 "How Gritty Are You?" quiz on page 101
SESSION 7 DATE 11/11	**SELF-TALK**	"Seeing the Rainbow in the Rainstorm" page 127
SESSION 8 DATE 11/18	**EVERYONE IS UNIQUE**	Unique Bingo game cards on page 144
SESSION 9 DATE 11/19	**TEACH OTHERS WHAT YOU KNOW** Post Survey	Questions for "Walk-About" on lanyards, page 157

Mindset Matters Group

Dear Parents/Guardians,

As part of our school's developmental counseling program, students are sometimes invited to participate in small group counseling experiences. Your child has been invited to join a group called MINDSET MATTERS. This group will meet once a week for thirty minutes and will last approximately eight weeks. The purpose of this group is to provide students with an opportunity to explore different ways to learn and how determination and positive thinking lead to better results. Students will participate in discussions, surveys and activities aimed at furthering the development of interpersonal and academic skills. It is my hope that this experience will support the social/emotional and academic growth of your child. If you have any questions, please feel free to call me at the number below. Thank you for your support and consideration. I look forward to getting to know your child better.

Sincerely,

School Counselor

Phone #_____

- ✂ - - -

Please sign and return to _____.

_____ Yes, my child_____, has my permission to participate.

_____ I prefer that my child not participate in the group.

_____   _____

Parent/Guardian Signature   Date

Mindset Matters
Pre-Post Survey

Student Name_____ Date_____

Circle if you are the **TEACHER** or **PARENT**

Directions: This survey will help me understand more about the strengths and weaknesses of each student. Answer on a scale of 1-5 how you would rate them. Thank you, and let me know if you have any questions.

	Strongly Agree	Agree	Not Sure	Disagree	Strongly Disagree
1. He/she has good study skills.	5	4	3	2	1
2. He/she has positive self-esteem.	5	4	3	2	1
3. He/she handles it appropriately if he/she makes mistakes.	5	4	3	2	1
4. He/she can calm down if angry.	5	4	3	2	1
5. He/she has a good attitude about school.	5	4	3	2	1
6. He/she could explain how his/her brain works.	5	4	3	2	1
7. He/she is determined and has a "don't give up" work ethic.	5	4	3	2	1

Mindset Matters
Student Pre-Survey (Grades 4-6)

	Strongly Agree	Agree	Not Sure	Disagree	Strongly Disagree
1. I can be anything I want to be when I grow up.	5	4	3	2	1
2. I am smart.	5	4	3	2	1
3. It is OK if I make mistakes.	5	4	3	2	1
4. I know how to calm down if I start getting angry.	5	4	3	2	1
5. People would say I have a good attitude.	5	4	3	2	1
6. I could teach others about how brains work.	5	4	3	2	1
7. I like school.	5	4	3	2	1
8. If I mess up on something, I immediately get frustrated.	5	4	3	2	1
9. I typically look on the bright side of things.	5	4	3	2	1
10. I have good study skills.	5	4	3	2	1
11. Other people like to have me on their team.	5	4	3	2	1
12. If I practice something long enough, I will finally get it.	5	4	3	2	1

Mindset Matters

Student Pre/Post Survey (Grades 2-4)

Name:_____ **Teacher:**_____

1. I can be anything I want to be when I grow up.	😊 😐 ☹️
2. I am smart.	😊 😐 ☹️
3. It is OK if I make mistakes.	😊 😐 ☹️
4. I know how to calm down if I start getting angry.	😊 😐 ☹️
5. People would say I have a good attitude.	😊 😐 ☹️
6. I could teach others about how brains work.	😊 😐 ☹️
7. If I practice something long enough, I will finally get it.	😊 😐 ☹️

Get your mind set to learn!

· ·

© National Center For Youth Issues • www.ncyi.org • 866-318-6294
Please refer to page 2 for duplication information

Group Reminder Cards

It's time for our group!

Your name _____

Day and Time _____

Location_____

It's time for our group!

Your name _____

Day and Time _____

Location_____

It's time for our group!

Your name _____

Day and Time _____

Location_____

It's time for our group!

Your name _____

Day and Time _____

Location_____

Mindset Matters for Classroom Curriculum

A Crosswalk of Possibilities

As you plan the scope and sequence of classroom guidance, look to see which lesson in each concept you might like to teach. You can teach this curriculum by covering a lesson in each concept. There are also lessons that can cover more than one concept.

Mindfulness	What Does it Mean to be Present? Page 50		Mindfulness Word Search Page 49	Mindful Minute Glitter Bottle Page 55	Mindfulness Quiz-Quiz Trade Page 59
Identify how your Brain Works	Start Your Ignition with Metacognition: The Brain Car Page 65	Mindful not Mind FULL Page 43	Licorice Connections Page 68	Brain Riddles Page 70	Neuro What Article Page 73
Not Yet is OK	Do You Get it Yet? Page 86	You Can Learn Anything: But at First, you might NOT YET Get It Page 84	Everyone Can Learn to Ride a Bicycle: The Power Of Yet Poem Page 90	Beautiful Oops Page 89	Leo Late Bloomer Page 80
Determination	Are you Determined to Crack the Code? Page 97	What To Do When You Get Stuck Page 110	Determination Interview Page 109	Perseverance Pipe Cleaners Page 99	Winners Never Quit: Goal Setting Page 103
Self-Talk	Positive Thinking = Growth Mindset Page 117	Positive Problem Solving Page 124	Seeing the Rainbow in the Rainstorm Page 127	The Dot Confidence vs. Competence Page 122	Tiger, Tiger is It True? Page 134
Everyone is Unique	We Are The Same, We are Different Page 138	Only One You Page 145	Unique Signature Bingo Page 144	Unique Word Search Page 143	Eggbert: All the Same on the Inside Page 149
Teach What You Know to Others	Go on a "Teach Others Walk-About" Page 157	Poster Making (one for each letter) Pages 17-23	Make your own Door Hanger Page 156	Choreograph your own Mindset Chant Page 13	Growth Mindset Tic-Tac-Toe Page 155

Record what Lessons You Did To Teach MINDSET

Grade Level _____

	What Lesson Do You Want To Teach for this Concept?
Mindfulness	
Identify how your Brain Works	
Not Yet is OK	
Determination	
Self-Talk	
Everyone is Unique	
Teach What You Know to Others	

Staff Professional Development

As you teach the concepts of Growth Mindset to students, you will find that teachers are interested in learning more about it, too. If you are interested in doing a book study or some staff professional development in this area, consider these ideas:

1. Get buy-in from administration. Consider sharing some of the video clips in the overview section on page 163 with them. Or buy/share with them the book, *Mindsets in the Classroom*, by Ricci.

2. Set up a time to meet with staff who are interested. Below is a sample email invitation.

Hello teachers!

Our administration wants to support us as we grow professionally, which is to say that they want us to use our professional learning time in the best way possible. They have invited us to get together and explore some research that some of us are familiar with at different levels. The concepts that we will be exploring are regarding "Growth Mindset." Want a bit more info? At our first meeting, we will watch this 10 minute TED talk video.

The Power of Believing You Can Improve
https://www.ted.com/talks/carol_dweck_the_power_of_believing_that_you_can_improve

The whole idea is about how mindfulness, grit, perseverance, doing challenging work, and understanding how the brain can grow, actually affects achievement scores and personal outcomes. How cool is that!

We'll meet in the _____ (place) at _____ (time). These meetings will be brief and informative. I am looking forward to growing our brains together.

Name

School Counselor
School

Mini-Grant Sample: Think About Applying for a Grant

Grants are typically available from a variety of sources including your school, your county, stores, PTA, and professional organizations. Here is a sample of a mini-grant to use as a guide.

2015-2016 Mini-Grant Request Form

NAME: _Lisa King_   **DATE:** _11-16-15_

CLASS OR SPECIAL AREA: _Counseling Department_   **TOTAL $ REQUESTED:** _$126.67_

PROJECT SUMMARY/REASON FOR REQUEST: *Growth Mindset is a theory developed by Dr. Carol Dweck at Stanford University. This theory is about teaching students that with effort, they can get smarter and grow their brains. It is powerful to tell kids that the research proves that kids who learn about Growth Mindset actually DO BETTER. Through this theory students learn about mindfulness, some basic facts about their brain, how important it is to have grit and determination, the power of self-talk, and how everyone learns at a different pace. Growth mindset promotes that intellect and innate talent are just the starting point; that one's ability can be developed through dedication and hard work. It is an exciting new theory for counselors to teach students so that students realize that they have the ability to grow their brains and find success in both academic and personal outcomes.*

HOW WILL THIS MINI GRANT BENEFIT ALL THE CHILDREN YOU TEACH (PLEASE BE SPECIFIC): *With the materials bought through this grant, I will develop lessons for grades 2-5 as well as lessons for small group counseling.*

MATERIALS NEEDED:

ITEM	VENDOR	QUANTITY	COST	TOTAL
Plush Neuron	Amazon.com	2	9.90	$19.80
Brain Erasers	Oriental Trading	2 (24 pieces)	5.50	$11.00
Young Genius BRAINS book	Amazon.com	8	6.99	$55.92
Race Car Assortment	Oriental Trading	1 (set of 30)	12.99	$12.99
Mindset: The New Psychology of Success by Carol Dweck	Amazon.com	1	16.00	$16.00
Fantastic Elastic Brain	Amazon.com	1	10.96	$10.96
TOTAL				$126.67

Mindset
Matters

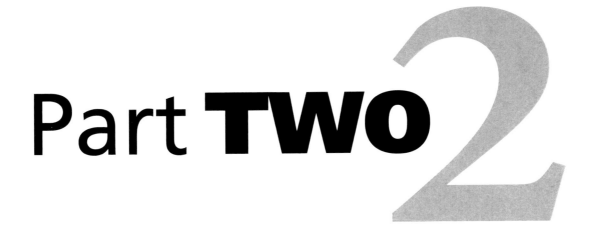

Part **TWO** 2

Mindset
Matters

Part **TWO** 2

Chapter 1
Mindfulness

Resources to Teach Mindfulness

Bibliotherapy List

The following books are great resources to supplement the lessons in this chapter on the subject of mindfulness.

What Does It Mean to Be Present?
by Rana DiOrio

A Handful of Quiet: Happiness in Four Pebbles
by Thich Nhat Hanh

Mindful Monkey Happy Panda
by Lauren Alderfer

Moody Cow Meditates
by Keri Lee MacLean

Peaceful Piggy Meditation
by Kerry Lee MacLean and Kerry MacLean

Silence
by Lemniscates

Sitting Still Like a Frog
by Eline Snel

You are a Lion
by Taeeun Yoo

Websites and Video Clips about Mindfulness

Mindfulness	URL	Age	Length
"Just Breathe" by Julie Bayer Salzman & Josh Salzman	https://www.youtube.com/watch?v=RVA2N6tX2cg	2nd to 6th	3:41
Mind in a Jar - Planting Seeds of Mindfulness MOVIE!	https://www.youtube.com/watch?v=QNmMH6tqiMc	4th-5th	1:13
JusTme - My Mindfulness	https://www.youtube.com/watch?v=JUKItN1Z8kw	2nd to 6th	2:38
JusTme Feat. E.E.D.E.E - Mindful or Nah	https://www.youtube.com/watch?v=JBRp2d7-X6k	2nd to 6th	4:15
Sesame Street: Common and Colbie Caillat - "Belly Breathe" with Elmo	https://www.youtube.com/watch?v=_mZbzDOpylA	2nd to 6th	2:25
JusTme Im Present	https://www.youtube.com/watch?v=XjlWFqvThBY	2nd to 6th	3:01
Yoga for Kids: Breathing Warm-Ups	https://www.youtube.com/watch?v=SEC0V8uU048	2nd to 6th	1:17

- **Mindfulschools.org (online course $100) done online**
- **Drchrisportherwillard.com**
- **Childmind.org**

> *The faculty of voluntarily bringing back a wandering attention over and over again, is the very root of judgement, character and will.*
>
> **William James**
> Principles of Psychology, 1890

Mindful NOT Mind FULL

This lesson was inspired by watching the following TED talk by Richard Burnett:

Mindfulness in Schools: Richard Burnett at TEDxWhitechapel
https://www.youtube.com/watch?v=6mlk6xD_xAQ.

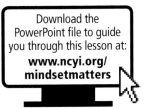
Download the PowerPoint file to guide you through this lesson at:
www.ncyi.org/ mindsetmatters

Materials

Download "MSM_PowerPoint 1,"
"True/False Cards" (page 46), "Mindful or Mind FULL" worksheet (page 48)

Procedures

1. Begin the lesson by telling the class we will play a true and false activity game and discuss answers afterwards.

2. Students are each given 2 cards (see page 46). When they hear each of the following statements, they should choose one of the answers to hold up showing you (at the front of the class) the answer. Record their answers for pre-post data. This also can be given in a paper/pencil form (page 47)

   a. I know a lot about how the brain works.

   b. I am interested in how the brain works.

   c. People that are smart at Math and Reading will get better careers when they are older.

   d. Your brain actually grows the more you practice different skills.

   e. When kids know about how their brain works, they actually do better in school.

   f. When you take a deep breath, your belly goes in.

3. Tell the group before we move on in the lesson let's all stand up. Tell students, "We are going to count to three all together when I say GO. For each number we say clap your hands as hard as you can. After you clap, put your hands out in front of you like you are holding a ball."

4. Then all together say "1,2,3" while clapping and then hold your hands apart in front of you.

5. Instruct the group to now focus on their hands. Say to the group, "Notice what you feel. Now put your attention on your thumbs. Now put your attention on your right pinkie."

....

6. Ask students to sit back down and raise their hands to describe what they were feeling.

7. After this exercise, show the slide on PowerPoint (or mini poster on page 45) of the Thinking versus the Sensing parts of the brain.

8. Tell the students that we were all just in a sensing state… a mindful state… where we were directing our attention to our hands in the here and now, to what we were feeling and to what was happening in the present.

9. Typically, we are using the THINKING part of our brain. Thinking is where we usually put our attention. We are often thinking about our friends, our plans, or our worries when we should have our brains on the teacher. We think about being hungry, what we should have done differently, what we will wear tomorrow, etc.

10. MANY times we are not living in our bodies but in our heads. Mindfulness is about being in the present. Mindful NOT Mind FULL.

11. Research has shown that we are HEALTHIER if we spend some time in the sensing state. This means minds are taking a moment to be in the present and not in the thinking state.

12. Does anyone know how we can practice being mindful (or in other words, being in tune to our sensing brain)?

13. Review ways to practice mindfulness (deep breathing, counting the sounds, going to your happy place, acknowledging your thoughts and moving on, or to concentrate very intently on the here and now (sometimes with music, or even coloring).

14. To end today's lesson we will complete the worksheet on page 48 to express what it means to be mindful and what usually fills our minds.

15. Distribute worksheet and conclude the lesson by asking students what they learned.

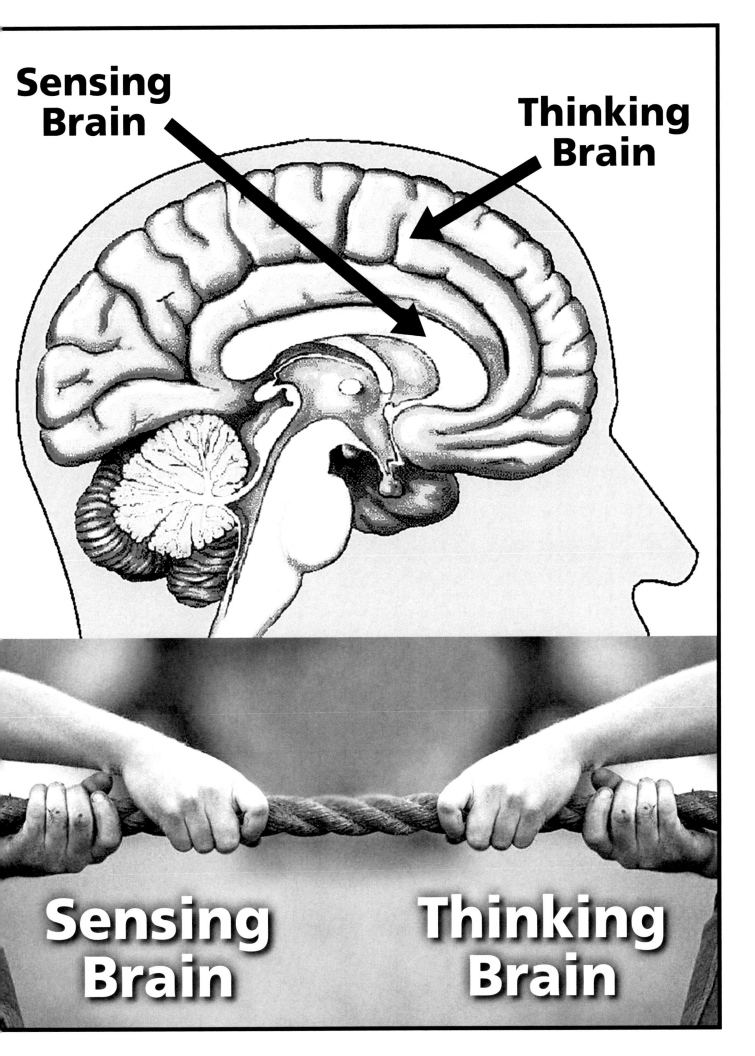

Sensing Brain

Thinking Brain

Sensing Brain

Thinking Brain

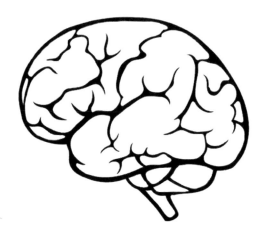

TRUE

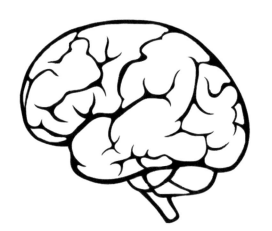

FALSE

TRUE OR FALSE?

Name _____

Directions

Read the statements below and circle whether you think the statements are TRUE or FALSE.

1. I know a lot about how
   the brain works.   **TRUE**   **FALSE**

2. I am <u>interested</u> in how
   the brain works.   **TRUE**   **FALSE**

3. People that are smart at Math
   and Reading will get better
   careers when they are older.   **TRUE**   **FALSE**

4. Your brain actually grows the
   more you practice different skills. **TRUE**   **FALSE**

5. When kids know about how
   their brain works, they actually
   do better in school.   **TRUE**   **FALSE**

6. When you take a deep breath,
   your belly goes in.   **TRUE**   **FALSE**

Name _____

Mindful *or* Mind FULL

Below, in the thought bubble labeled **MIND FULL**, draw what fills your mind throughout the day. What are activities you think about, questions you think, and worries that cross your mind? Go through your day and fill the bubble with all of the things that might enter your thoughts in a day. In the other thought bubble labeled **MINDFUL**, draw what mindfulness means to you. You can draw a peaceful scene that you think about when you are trying to still your mind or some of the mindfulness practices we have discussed.

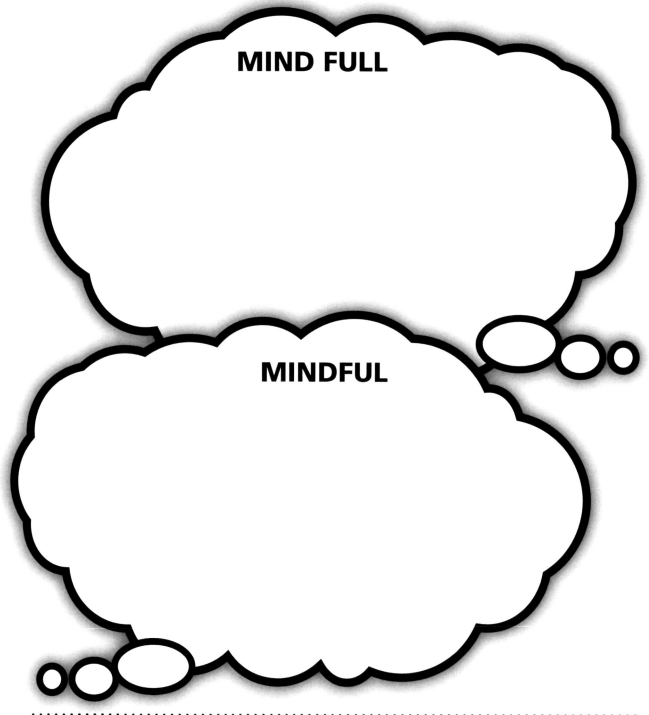

Mindfulness Word Search

Name _____

Directions: All of the words below have to do with "MINDFULNESS." How many can you find?

```
A  K  L  K  Q  A  C  C  E  P  T  A  N  C  E
I  T  Z  E  S  Y  B  P  T  R  J  U  P  G  J
X  N  T  T  V  R  F  S  A  U  X  S  R  N  Z
R  G  I  E  E  E  D  B  R  Z  S  K  A  I  Z
I  L  A  A  N  N  I  E  T  E  D  N  C  S  S
L  G  T  J  U  T  K  L  N  B  A  Q  T  N  I
H  H  W  O  V  C  I  L  E  H  I  P  I  E  U
E  W  S  F  D  H  U  O  C  B  L  L  C  S  S
K  U  J  W  I  F  S  M  N  X  Y  F  E  S  Z
H  X  J  D  D  U  S  N  O  T  I  C  E  X  K
J  A  L  N  N  A  Z  V  C  F  Q  A  Z  O  H
Y  C  I  T  N  E  S  E  R  P  O  F  G  L  L
B  M  L  W  D  H  C  A  P  P  E  C  C  O  U
T  E  I  U  Q  V  L  S  Y  T  V  D  U  X  Y
J  T  I  R  G  R  Y  C  L  A  Q  Z  B  S  K
```

ACCEPTANCE	ATTENTION	BELIEVE
BREATHE	CONCENTRATE	DAILY
FOCUS	MINDFULNESS	NOTICE
PRACTICE	PRESENT	QUIET
SENSING	SOUNDS	STILL

© National Center For Youth Issues • www.ncyi.org • 866-318-6294
Please refer to page 2 for duplication information

What Does It Mean To Be Present?

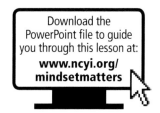

Download the PowerPoint file to guide you through this lesson at:
www.ncyi.org/ mindsetmatters

Materials

A prop of a gift/present, *What Does it Mean to be Present?* by Rana Diorio, Bag labeled "Distractions" with cards cut out (page 52), Download "MSM_PowerPoint 2," copies of worksheet "What Does It Mean to be Present?" (page 53), glue, scissors, crayons, pencil, and these videos:

Sesame Street: Common and Colbie Caillat - "Belly Breathe" with Elmo
https://www.youtube.com/watch?v=_mZbzDOpylA

JusTme Im Present
https://www.youtube.com/watch?v=XjlWFqvThBY

Procedures

1. Introduce your prop of a wrapped gift/present. Ask the class what this is. Someone will answer, "a present".

2. Tell the group that you are going to read a story about what it means to be present which doesn't mean you're going to be wrapped up like a gift!

3. Being present means being here and now. Tell students, "Before we read the story, who can think of a time you have been distracted? (Current distractions can be pointed out.)

4. Show the group a bag labeled DISTRACTIONS. Inside this bag are different things that keep us from paying attention to the here and now. Tell students that you will act out a distraction and see if they can guess what it is (use examples from cards on page 52). Have student volunteers come up and pull a card from the bag and act out more of these distractions.

Tell students that when they hear you (or the teacher) say "Be Present," it is a cue for them to put their hands on their stomachs and slowly breathe in and out. Breath in through the nose and out through the mouth, feeling your belly expand when you inhale. (Have students practice this as you read.)

5. Read to the class *What Does it Mean to Be Present?* by Rana Diorio.

6. After you read the book, review what it means to be present, also known as being mindful, by showing the PowerPoint (MSM_PowerPoint 2). Remind students that when they hear the cue "Be Present," they should put their hands on their bellies and focus on breathing.

50

7. Tell students they will be completing the worksheet (they can choose if they want to do Choice 1 or Choice 2 assignment). Show sample.

Choice 1:

a. Cut out each picture on the bottom of the worksheet.

b. Glue each picture onto the worksheet in the order of how meaningful each is to being present.

c. Fill in the sentence below to tell why being present is important.

Choice 2:

a. Cut out each picture on the bottom of the worksheet.

b. Choose 3 or more of these pictures to glue onto the worksheet.

c. Write a sentence about how this picture represents being present.

d. Fill in the sentence below to tell why being present is important.

8. Have students share why they think being present is important. Play one of the two options while children are working on this assignment (these are hyperlinked on "MSM_ PowerPoint 2").

Option1:
Sesame Street: Common and Colbie Caillat - "Belly Breathe" with Elmo
https://www.youtube.com/watch?v=_mZbzDOpylA

Option2:
JusTme Im Present
https://www.youtube.com/watch?v=XjlWFqvThBY

Extension

For a list, description and picture of yoga poses for children, visit:

58 Yoga Poses for Kids
http://www.kidsyogastories.com/kids-yoga-poses/

Distractions

HUNGER

TEXTING ON A CELL PHONE

DAY-DREAMING

HEARING LOUD NOISES

PLAYING WITH THINGS IN YOUR DESK

FEELING MAD

What Does It Mean To Be Present?

Being present in the here and now is important because:

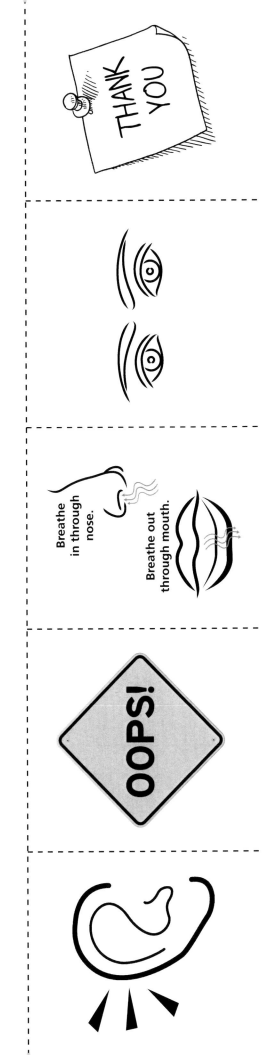

 **and be mindful.**

Sit still with silence.

Take a deep breath.

Observe what you see and hear.

Put all thoughts out of your mind.

Mindfulness is…
paying attention in a particular way.

Mindfulness is …
noticing what is happening right now.

Mindful Minute Bottle

Materials

Warm Water, Clear Elmer's Glue, Empty Water Bottles, Food Coloring, Glitter, and "Mindful Minute Bottle" labels (page 56). Optional materials: glitter glue tube, Mod Podge®, tissue paper.

Mindful Minute Bottles are made with 10-20% glue, 80-90% water, and as much glitter as you want. Allow for a little bit of room at the top in case you need more water or glue. This lesson is best done in a small group rather than classroom lesson, but could be done in either. This can be done over one or two group sessions.

Directions

1. Show students one of the following videos:

   Mind in a Jar - Planting Seeds of Mindfulness MOVIE!
   https://www.youtube.com/watch?v=QNmMH6tqiMc

   "Just Breathe" by Julie Bayer Salzman & Josh Salzman
   https://www.youtube.com/watch?v=RVA2N6tX2cg

2. After watching the video, show students a model of a Mindful Minute Bottle. Tell them, "The glitter is like the thoughts in your mind. This bottle/jar can be used to calm down and take deep breaths until your thoughts have settled, just as the glitter settles to the bottom of the bottle.

3. Distribute a sturdy, empty water bottle to each student.

4. Have enough bottles of clear Elmer's glue available for 2 students to share, and instruct students to squirt/pour Elmer's clear glue into their water bottles. Students should fill about 10-20% of the bottle with the glue.

5. Have students add warm water. The easiest way to do this is if you have a warm water faucet that students can use directly from the spicket. If not, prepare a pitcher of warm water to have ready, and a filter to easily pour it into the water bottle (funnels are helpful.)

6. Add food coloring SPARINGLY. The water should be lighter rather than darker.

7. Finally, add as much loose glitter and/or glitter glue as you would like.

8. Close the top of the water bottle and shake, then take bottle top off until totally cooled.

9. Once it has cooled, put the lid back on and secure it with a hot glue gun.

10. Glue a "Mindful Minute Bottle" label (page 56) on the top of the bottle.

11. An optional step is to decorate the bottles with tissue paper and Mod Podge®.

Mindful Minute Bottle Labels

MINDFUL MINUTE   MINDFUL MINUTE   MINDFUL MINUTE   MINDFUL MINUTE   MINDFUL MINUTE

MINDFUL MINUTE   MINDFUL MINUTE   MINDFUL MINUTE   MINDFUL MINUTE   MINDFUL MINUTE

MINDFUL MINUTE   MINDFUL MINUTE   MINDFUL MINUTE   MINDFUL MINUTE   MINDFUL MINUTE

MINDFUL MINUTE   MINDFUL MINUTE   MINDFUL MINUTE   MINDFUL MINUTE   MINDFUL MINUTE

MINDFUL MINUTE   MINDFUL MINUTE   MINDFUL MINUTE   MINDFUL MINUTE   MINDFUL MINUTE

Mindfulness is simply being aware of what is right now without wishing it were different.

Enjoying the pleasant without holding on when it changes. (which it will)

Being with the unpleasant without fearing it will always be this way. (which it won't)

–James Baraz
www.verybestquotes.com

56

© National Center For Youth Issues • www.ncyi.org • 866-318-6294
Please refer to page 2 for duplication information

Date:

Dear Parent/Guardian,

We have been having a great time in small group learning about mindfulness and creating our **MINDFUL MINUTE** Bottles. Mindfulness, or the practice of being in the here and now, has been found to help students calm down, be more focused, and assist in decision-making. These Mindful Minute Bottles were a fun way to teach the students new skills, like deep breathing and using self-control. Your child can shake the bottle, take deep breaths and watch the glitter settle in the bottle, just as their thoughts settle in their minds, so they can focus. There are two videos that explain these concepts, and watching them with your child would be a great way to get some conversations started (websites listed below). I hope this group activity was meaningful for your child.

Sincerely,

School Counselor

Check out these videos that we watched in group:

"Just Breathe" by Julie Bayer Salzman & Josh Salzman
https://www.youtube.com/watch?v=RVA2N6tX2cg

Mind in a Jar - Planting Seeds of Mindfulness MOVIE!
https://www.youtube.com/watch?v=QNmMH6tqiMc

. . . .

Name _____

What is Mindfulness?

Directions

Read the following article and then answer the questions below.

Student Article

What does it mean to be mindful? Being mindful which is also called "Mindfulness" means being aware of your surroundings and trying to focus on the here and now. When you are paying attention to your actions and feelings in a very "on purpose" way, you are being mindful. Some people think that to practice mindfulness you should try not to think about the future or the past, but you should concentrate on the present… the here and now. For example, you might think about the things you see and hear around you. This can be difficult if you are having a problem or having strong feelings. When we are having strong feelings, our brains go a mile a minute, so focusing on the present can be extremely hard. This is one reason it is important to practice mindfulness not only during tough times, but at times when everything is going OK, so that when things get rough you are in the habit of staying mindful. Practicing mindfulness means deep breathing, focusing on the moment we are in, and trying to be OK with whatever feelings we are having.

Questions

1. What does mindfulness mean?

_____

_____

_____

2. What are some ways to practice mindfulness?

_____

_____

_____

58

Mindfulness Quiz-Quiz Trade

Materials
"Quiz-Quiz Trade Cards" (page 60), bell

Procedures

1. Distribute the question cards (page 60) so that each student has one in his/her hand.

2. Instruct students to find a partner and stand face to face/toe to toe.

3. Student 1 asks Student 2 the question written on the card, and Student 2 answers.

4. Student 2 then asks Student 1 the question written on their card, and Student 2 answers.

5. Student 1 and Student 2 trade cards.

6. Have a signal or bell to notify students when it is time to trade cards and find a new partner.

Mindfulness Activity Cards
For Quiz-Quiz-Trade

Take a deep breath in through your nose and hold it for 6 seconds. Let it out through your mouth.

Name 3 things you see around you right now.

Say this out loud: "Mindfulness means seeing things in the here and now."

Tell what mindfulness means.

Stand up and stretch your arms out to the side as far as you can.

Sit crisscross with your hands on your knees and breathe in and out through your nose for 2 deep breaths.

Stand tall and lift one knee to the side and put your foot by your ankle. (this is the start of tree pose in yoga)

Put your hand on your tummy. Take a deep breath in. Concentrate on your tummy going out while you breathe out.

See if you can touch the floor by standing, bending from the waist and reaching down without bending your knees.

Be silent for 5 seconds and count as many sounds as you can that you hear.

What are 2 things that distract you from doing homework?

Why is being mindful important?

Mindset Matters

Part TWO 2
Chapter 2

Identify Brain Basics

Resources for Identifying Brain Basics

Bibliotherapy List

The following books are great resources to supplement the lessons in this chapter on the subject of understanding how the brain works.

Your Fantastic Elastic Brain
by Joann Deak

Think, Think, Think: Learning About Your Brain
by Pamela Hill Nettleton

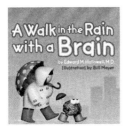
A Walk in the Rain with a Brain
by Edward Hallowell and Bill Mayer

Young Genius: Brains
by Kate Lennard

Websites about Brain Basics

www.kizoomlabs.com/products/brainventures/

www.teacher.scholastic.com/products/mindup/pdfs/MindUP_3-5_Sample_Poster.pdf

www.teacher.scholastic.com/products/mindup/pdfs/MindUP_K-2_Sample_Poster.pdf

www.edutopia.org/blog/neuroscience-behind-stress-and-learning-judy-willis

Video Clips about Brain Basics

Identify How Your Brain Works	URL	Length
How To Remember Stuff for Exams (A Brain Like a Sieve)	https://www.youtube.com/watch?v=kQ4Qw0-XnR4	1:33
How We Learn - Synapses and Neural Pathways	www.youtube.com/watch?v=t4np5wLAhWw	3:15
Your Brain is Plastic	www.youtube.com/watch?v=5KLPxDtMqe8	4:08
Structure of a Neuron	www.youtube.com/watch?v=Ta_vWUsrjho	6:00
How Youth Learn: Ned's GR8 8	https://www.youtube.com/watch?v=p_BskcXTqpM	6:12
Brain Jump with Ned the Neuron: Challenges Grow Your Brain	www.youtube.com/watch?v=g7FdMi03CzI	1:51
Brain Tricks - This Is How Your Brain Works	https://www.youtube.com/watch?v=JiTz2i4VHFw	4:40
How the Brain Works	https://www.youtube.com/watch?v=Y4O_Wkv66b0	1:36
The Learning Brain	www.youtube.com/watch?v=cgLYkV689s4&tlist=PL4111402B45D1OAFCgtindex=12	7:01
Neuroplasticity	www.youtube.com/watch?v=ELpfYCZa87gSindex=628.clist=PLfM-YIRNOOtoPuUcmpGa2avM16Q0YtbUi	2:03

64

Start Your Ignition with *Metacognition:*
The Brain Car

Metacognition is "thinking about thinking." Thinking is essential in school and life, so it is important to learn about learning and think about thinking.

Materials

Miniature cars (available at orientaltrading.com or many dollar stores), erasers in the shape of a brain (available at orientaltrading.com), hot glue gun

Procedures

1. Ask the students, "When you are in a car, can you see who is driving? Yes, usually you can see. If your body is a car, who is the boss/driver of that car? Yes, you are the driver of your own car, and your brain tells you when to stop, start, turn, etc. Yet, sometimes you have a race car brain and bicycle brakes. You have to train the brain to use those brakes."

2. Distribute miniature cars and brains (one to each student).

3. Counselor can hot glue the brain on top of the car as a symbol for you being in charge of yourself.

4. Discuss self-control with students.

5. Play Red Light, Green Light with students to symbolize how your brain tells you when to stop or go.

YOU ARE THE CAR, *and*
YOUR BRAIN IS THE DRIVER.

Sample Parent Letter to Send Home with the Brain Car

Date:

Dear Parent/Guardian,

I have enjoyed working with your child in our small group. Recently we made this craft project as a symbol of our discussion: "Your Brain is the Driver of YOU". We discussed the metaphor of, "If you are the car, your brain is the driver making the decisions of when to start and stop, and which way to turn. You and your brain make the decisions about your behavior and how you handle problems that come your way." We did some activities to further show how we are in control of our own actions. We've played games, read stories, and watched some video clips of understanding our brains and how positive thinking can help in most situations (whether they are problems we can control, or problems that are out of our control.)

I share this information with you so that you know some of the language we've used in our group and have some good discussions with your child about the topics we've discussed. Please feel free to call me if you have any feedback or questions.

Sincerely,

Lisa King, Ed.S, LPC
School Counselor
(678) 494-7603 x231

Don't forget to email your teachers to keep them in the loop about what you are doing with your small group students!

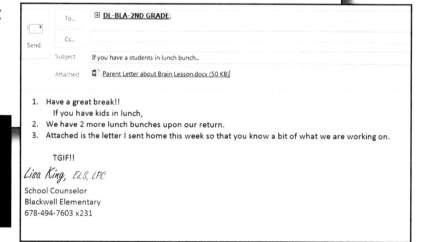

Name _____

Brain Maze

Directions

Your brain controls your thinking, so let it drive you through this maze. Start your engines and get to the finish line!

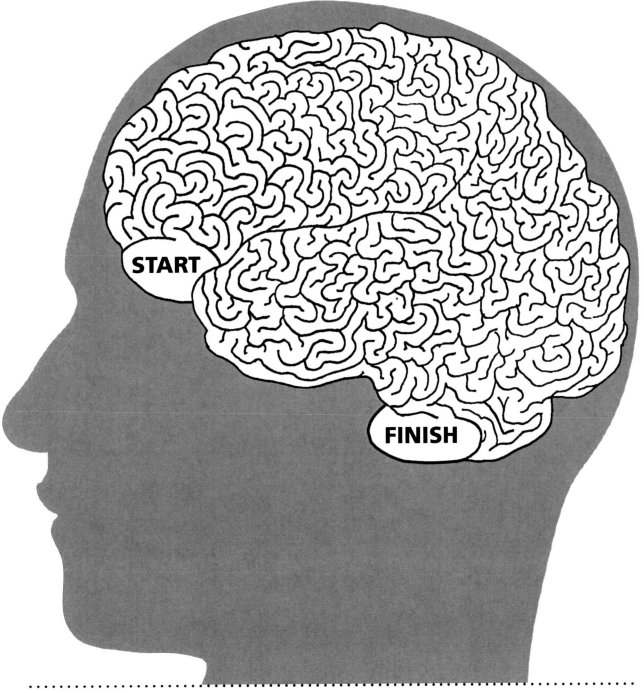

Licorice Connections:
Brain Food, A Yummy Lesson

Download the PowerPoint file to guide you through this lesson at:
www.ncyi.org/ mindsetmatters

Materials

"Licorice Connections" worksheet (page 69), Pull and Peel Licorice, "Fancy Facts about the Brain" (page 71), "Mindset Chant" (page 13), "Brain Riddles" (page 70), Download "MSM_ PowerPoint 3" and video:

How We Learn - Synapses and Neural Pathways
https://www.youtube.com/watch?v=t4np5wLAhWw

Procedures

1. Tell the students that in this lesson, we are talking about brain basics. Ask who knows any facts about the brain? Show "Fancy Facts about the Brain" mini-poster (page 71).

2. Teach students (if they don't already know) the "Mindset Chant" (page 13).

3. Show "Brain Riddles" (page 70) to the students and review. Once you train your brain to the type of riddles, they become easier to solve.

4. Growth Mindset is the study that scientists have done that found that kids who know more about their brain and embrace challenges tend to do better. So…let's learn.

5. Show students "MSM_PowerPoint 3." On slide #4, there is an icon hyperlinked to the video *How We Learn - Synapses and Neural Pathways,* **https://www.youtube.com/ watch?v=t4np5wLAhWw**.

6. After the video, introduce the yummy lesson we are doing which reinforces what the video taught us; our brain gets stronger by practicing skills. Within our brain are little roadways (or neural pathways) that get wider and stronger as you practice skills.

7. Distribute "Licorice Connections" worksheet (page 69) and Pull and Peel Licorice to each student.

8. Explain and model that students will trace the shape of the brain pathway with their Pull and Peel licorice. Showing that the skinny path is "Not Yet" putting one thin strip of licorice here and then make your licorice match the shape. Repeat for "I'm Starting to Understand" and "I've Got This." Then students will write examples of personal skills for each category in the spaces below the licorice model.

9. Then, of course students can eat their brain pathways.

Extension: Brain Gelatin Molds can be purchased to add fun and interest to your lessons. Make gelatin molds of the brain to serve to your students. Try different flavors and colors!

68

Name _____

Licorice Connections...Yum!

There are yummy ways to learn about the brain. Gross, you say? Well, yes it might be gross to talk about an "eating the brain" activity. But you know it will be an activity that you will always remember! And we are not really eating the brain, we are just going to imagine that this licorice represents our brain's pathways.

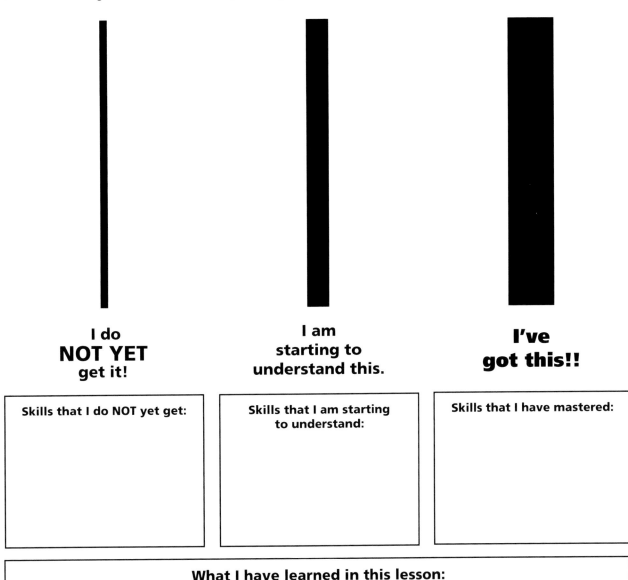

**I do
NOT YET
get it!**

**I am
starting to
understand this.**

**I've
got this!!**

Skills that I do NOT yet get:

**Skills that I am starting
to understand:**

Skills that I have mastered:

What I have learned in this lesson:

Brain Riddles

Here are some brain riddles. Try to figure out what the phrase is. At first it might be tricky, but like all things, when you train your brain, you can accomplish great things.

───── **Brain Riddle 1** ─────

Ban/ana

───── **Brain Riddle 2** ─────

YouJustMe

───── **Brain Riddle 3** ─────

stand
i

───── **Brain Riddle 4** ─────

GGEGEG

Answers

1. BANANA SPLIT   2. JUST BETWEEN YOU AND ME   3. I UNDERSTAND   4. SCRAMBLED EGGS

Fancy Facts about
the BRAIN!

QUESTION

Why does the brain have so many folds?

ANSWER

Those folds create more surface area for you to think. If you laid out those folds, your brain would be as large as a newspaper page.

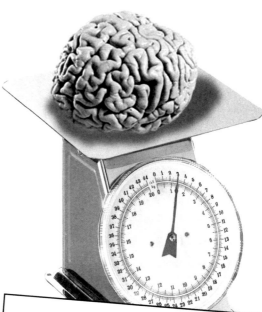

QUESTION

How much does an adult brain weigh?

ANSWER

Approximately 3 pounds.

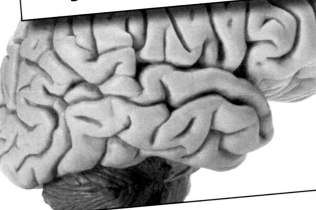

QUESTION

How fast do the signals go from one set of neurons to another when you have a thought?

ANSWER

About 680 miles an hour— the speed of an airplane.

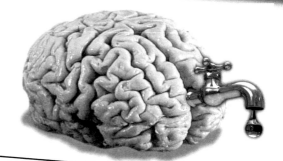

QUESTION

How much of the brain is made up of water.

ANSWER

The brain is 75% water.

Name _____

Brain Power Puzzle

Directions

Solve the crossword puzzle below to learn about brain basics.

For help in solving the puzzle, watch the video *The Learning Brain*
https://www.youtube.com/watch?v=cgLYkV689s4&t-list=PL4111402B45D10AFCgtindex=12

Across

3. Repeating a skill over and over

6. Looking on the _____ of things is another way to think about positive self-talk.

8. Brain cells are called_____.

Down

1. You need to train your _____ to learn different skills.

2. When something is difficult to accomplish it is a _____.

4. The feeling of frustration that can get in the way of thinking clearly.

5. You can get dehydrated if your brain does not get enough _____.

7. Neuroplasticity is a fancy way to say that your brain can _____ as you learn new skills.

Name _____

Neuro What??

NEUROPLASTICITY. Now that is a hard word to say! Let's break it down. *Neuro-plas-ti-city.* It is a tough word to say but a very cool idea to understand. The idea of neuroplasticity is that the brain is not fixed in size and shape, but it can actually grow. You can become smarter and better at different skills with practice. Some people think Michael Jordan was born with all the ability he needed to be an amazing basketball player, but we have learned that it was practice and determination that allowed him to be an all-time great at that sport. Scientists have learned that all of our brains can get better at our skills the more we practice, too.

You see, our brain has these little tiny cells called neurons and these neurons are looking for a path to send a message to other parts of our brain. There are approximately 100 billion neurons in the human brain with the chance to create more and more. The more we practice a skill, the more our brain is changing that little path into a sturdy roadway through our brain to make doing that skill easier.

Questions

How can we get smarter and better at a skill?

_____

_____

Was Michael Jordan born having all of his skills, or did he have to practice in order to become a great basketball player?

_____

What are the cells in the brain called?

_____

Still interested? Watch the video *Neuroplasticity*:
https://www.youtube.com/watch?v=ELpfYCZa87gSkindex=628.clist=PLfM-YIRNOOtoPu UcmpGa2avMl6Q0YtbUi

---

BONUS POINTS! Take this home and discuss 2 things that you learned from this article with someone at your house. Have them sign below.

Signature of Adult : _____

NEURONS and AXONS and DENDRITES...OH MY!
LEARNING GUIDE

Your brain has teeny tiny cells called neurons. These cells grow, multiply and help to make you smarter.

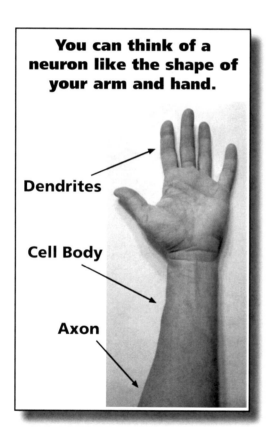

You can think of a neuron like the shape of your arm and hand.

Dendrites

Cell Body

Axon

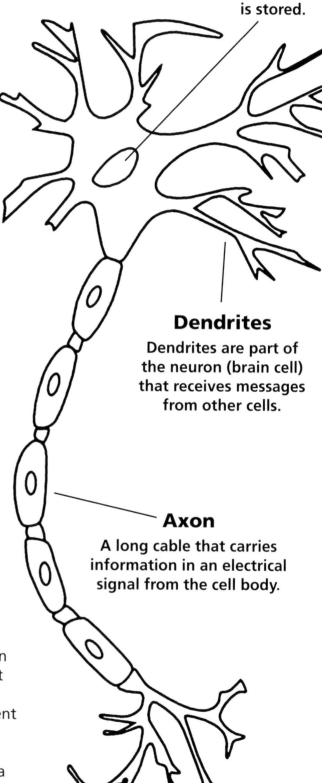

Cell Body
Where information is stored.

Dendrites
Dendrites are part of the neuron (brain cell) that receives messages from other cells.

Axon
A long cable that carries information in an electrical signal from the cell body.

There are approximately 100 billion neurons in the human brain. 100,000,000,000 !! Hold out your arm and spread your fingers. Your hand represents the "cell body;" your fingers represent "dendrites" bringing information to the cell body; your arm represents the "axon" taking information away from the cell body. Here is a model of what a real neuron looks like.

For a great printout of brain information, see
http://teacher.scholastic.com/products/mindup/pdfs/MindUP_3-5_Sample_Poster.pdf

Name _____

NEURONS and AXONS
and DENDRITES...OH MY!

Label the parts of a neuron.

1. _____

2. _____

3. _____

Here are things I learned about how the brain works.

Write answers inside the space below.

_____

_____

_____

_____

_____

_____

Mindset *Matters*

Part **TWO** 2

Chapter 3

Not Yet is OK

Rivers know this: there is no hurry. We shall get there someday.
– A.A. Milne, Winnie-the-Pooh

Resources to Teach Not Yet Is OK
(The Power of Not Yet)

Bibliotherapy List

The following books are great resources to supplement the lessons in this chapter on the subject of understanding the concept of *Not Yet* and *The Power of Yet*.

 Everyone Can Learn to Ride a Bicycle by Chris Raschka

 Beautiful Oops by Barney Salzberg

 I Will Never Not Ever Eat a Tomato by Lauren Child

 *Leo the Late Bloomer* by Robert Kraus

 Emily's Art by Peter Catalanotto

 The OK Book by Amy Krouse Rosenenthal and Tom Lichtenheld

 Thanks for the Feedback (I Think) by Julia Cook

 *Sergio Makes a Splash* by Edel Rodriguez

 *Rosie Sprout's Time to Shine* by Allison Wortche

Video Clips about Not Yet

Not Yet is OK (The Power of Yet)	URL	Length
Famous Failures	https://www.youtube.com/watch?v=zLYECIjmnQs	1:18
You Can Learn Anything	https://www.youtube.com/watch?v=JC82Il2cjqA	1:30
Jesse Ruben-We Can-OFFICIAL Music Video	https://www.youtube.com/watch?v=59Aj9E5lCn0	4:11
Barney Saltzberg's Beautiful Oops, full video	https://www.youtube.com/watch?v=B0A3QhGVyDs	9:59
Sesame Street: Janelle Monae - Power of Yet	https://www.youtube.com/watch?v=XLeUvZvuvAs	2:42
Understanding Talent	https://www.youtube.com/watch?v=LfUvchfrcS0	2:12

Leo the Late Bloomer

Materials

Leo The Late Bloomer by Robert Kraus, "Power of Yet" poster (page 81), "I CAN" worksheet (page 82), "NOT YET" worksheet (page 83)

Procedures

1. Read the book *Leo the Late Bloomer* by Robert Krauss.

2. Review the book by discussing how we all learn at a different pace.

3. Have the children turn to a partner. Tell them to "discuss something you are good at doing and something your partner is good at doing."

Then think of something that you both are working on learning but you can't do. Instruct students to say, "I can't do _____" then have them add the word yet to the end of the sentence. "I can't do _____ YET." Refer to "Power of Yet" poster (page 81).

4. Have students discuss with their partner, "In what ways do you hope to bloom and grow this year?"

5. Express to students that they will bloom just like a flower.
Use the analogy of how flowers in the same garden grow at different speeds. Use a flower or plant as a visual.

6. Distribute a double-sided "I CAN" and "NOT YET" worksheet (page 82 on one side and page 83 on the other). Discuss the Power of Yet. You can use the "Power of Yet" mini-poster (page 81). You may optionally hang a copy of the mini-poster in the room.

7. Instruct students to color in the worksheets with words and pictures that represent what they can do (on "I CAN") and what they have not yet learned (on "NOT YET").

The Power of YET

If you are thinking

"I don't get it!"

or

"I can't do this!"

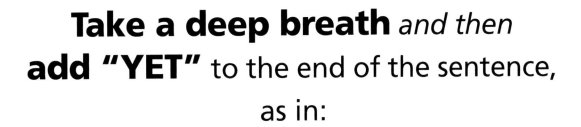

Take a deep breath *and then*
add "YET" to the end of the sentence,
as in:

I don't get it...YET.
I can't do this...YET.

**It may not be easy, but you
are up for the challenge, and
you will eventually get it!!**

Name _____

Directions

Decorate this I CAN with words or pictures that describe skills that you have learned but at one time you didn't know. Use words or pictures that describe skills that you have not yet learned, that you are working on, or hopeful to one day have.

Name _____

Directions

Decorate this NOT YET with words or pictures that describe skills that you have learned but at one time you didn't know. Use words or pictures that describe skills that you have not yet learned, that you are working on, or hopeful to one day have.

You Can Learn Anything: But at First, You Might NOT YET Get It

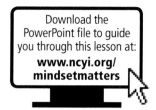

Download the PowerPoint file to guide you through this lesson at: **www.ncyi.org/ mindsetmatters**

Materials

Download "MSM_PowerPoint 4," "Mindset Chant" (page 13), Rubric for Do You Get It Yet?" worksheet (page 87), "Which Step Have You Reached Today?" (page 88), "Games: Do You Get it Yet?" (page 86) and videos:

You Can Learn Anything
https://www.youtube.com/watch?v=JC82Il2cjqA

Brain Jump with Ned the Neuron: Challenges Grow Your Brain
https://www.youtube.com/watch?v=g7FdMi03CzI

Procedures

This follows the PPT titled, "MSM_PowerPoint 4," downloaded from the website.

1. "Today's lesson is to teach you that you can learn anything, and I'm going to prove it to you."

2. Tell the students you will start by learning the "Mindset Chant" (page 13). Have this displayed on a projector or make copies so that the words can be seen. Explain to them, "I will be the Leader, and you respond as the Class. As we go through this I will teach you the motions."

LEADER: Whatcha gotta do?
CLASS: I've got to train my brain.

MOTION: Make a muscle and then point to brain.

LEADER: Why you gotta do it?
CLASS: Gotta show the world.

MOTION: Hand over eyes, like you are searching

LEADER: Whatcha gonna show them?
CLASS: That I've got some skills.

MOTION: Point to yourself with both thumbs

LEADER: What kind of skills?
CLASS: Whatever I work on!

MOTION: Wag pointer finger at someone and say in a silly voice

LEADER: What's that called?
CLASS: Growth Mindset, Growth Mindset, Growth Mindset

MOTION: Do a little dance

3. Tell the students, "Now that we have learned this chant. Let's learn what it means. There is new research about this thing called Growth Mindset that proves you can become smarter depending on how much you practice a skill and how you handle challenges."

4. Write "NOT YET" on the board. Tell students that scientists at Stanford University have studied something called the "power of yet," and they have discovered how to make people the smartest they can be. They have found that we have all been in a place where you don't get something yet. Where you **NOT YET** get it. (In fact, Dr. Dweck suggests that a more suitable grade for teachers to give students is "Not Yet" in lieu of an F).

5. Review with students that there are many things we have learned but couldn't do at first: Walking, Reading, Multiplication, Video Games. You lived in "Not Yet" when you were learning, and scientists have learned that it is important how you deal with **NOT YET** that matters.

6. Show your students this video:
Brain Jump with Ned the Neuron: Challenges Grow Your Brain
https://www.youtube.com/watch?v=g7FdMi03CzI.

In this video you will meet Ned the Neuron who teaches us about how you can get smarter by training your brain. When you say train the brain make the motion that goes along with the chant (make a muscle and then point to your brain.)

7. After watching the video, ask the class if they want to play a game. Tell them that everyone (even the teachers) will live in "Not Yet" until they get the trick. The game goes like this:

LEADER SAYS: "I am going on a picnic and I am bringing a (say an item that starts with the first letter of your last name.) Who else would like to come on the picnic?"

STUDENTS ANSWER: "I am bringing a _____ "

LEADER: Tell students they can go on the picnic with you. The trick is that they can come along if they say they are bringing an item that starts with the first letter of their first name. For example: Ms. King can bring a Kitten (I use my last name), Susan can bring String, Adam can bring an Apple. I also emphasize the sound of the first letter of the name and then the object when I say what I am bringing.

LEADER: Remind group that they are living in **NOT YET**, if they don't get it. It is like when you don't understand a math concept and the person next to you does. How do you handle NOT YET? Are you frustrated? Embarrassed to admit you don't understand? Eventually you can tell the students the trick to the game.

8. Explain that everyone knows what it feels like to not get something yet, but the truth is that everyone can learn anything, and the experts agree.

9. Show the video: *You Can Learn Anything*
https://www.youtube.com/watch?v=JC82Il2cjqA

10. Show graphic on slide 13 from "MSM_PowerPoint 4" and/or handout "Rubric for Do You Get It Yet?" worksheet (page 87) and "Which Step Have You Reached Today?" (page 88).

11. Have students stand up and do the "Mindset Chant" (page 13). Invite the students to create their own moves to the chant.

For more games that reinforce this point, see "Games: Do You Get it Yet?" (page 86)

Refer to the Mini Posters on page 87 or 88 to demonstrate different levels of "getting it" if students get frustrated.

Games: Do You Get it YET?

"YET" is a concept of Carol Dweck's, "Growth Mindset." It is an important and awesome concept that promotes learners becoming comfortable with knowing that they might not "YET" get a concept. When you do "NOT YET" understand something…this is where learning takes place. Those with a growth mindset embrace a challenge, knowing that mistakes lead to success and that learning is a process.

Below are activities that can be done in small group or classroom lessons. These are activities that I learned at camp and perfectly show how a non-academic challenge can lead to the frustration and celebration of learning.

The following games/activities are fun ways to teach the concept of "Not Yet". Each activity has a "trick" that the audience will need to catch onto in order to achieve success.

Activity 1
Going to the Moon

Directions for leader: Tell students that this is a game where you have to say that you are bringing the correct items in order to come to the moon. I can bring a spoon but not a fork. (The trick is that you say I can bring "something with double letters" but I can't bring "something without double letters." I can bring a glass but not a cup. I can bring a mitten but not a glove. To make it easier, you can accentuate the double letter sound. I can bring a "spooooooooon" I can bring a "mitttttttten." Let students try to say what they can bring on our trip to the moon and see who can come along.

Activity 2
I Can Do the Broom Dance

Directions for leader: Grab a broom and hold it in any way you would like. Sing this as a song, or say it as a sing-song like poem "I can do the broom dance, broom dance, broom dance, I can do the broom dance how 'bout you?" The trick is that the leader clears his/her throat each time before doing the dance and song. It doesn't matter really how you sing it or what dance you do… as long as you clear your throat first. If someone else does it with the trick you tell them, YES you do know how to do the broom dance. Eventually you might have to accentuate the "Ahhhhhhheeeeeem. I can do the broom dance, broom dance, broom dance, I can do the broom dance how 'bout you?" Allow students to do their version to try and do it correctly.

Rubric for Do You Get It Yet?

4	3	2	1
I can show others how to do this.	I can do this all by myself.	I need more practice	I need help.

Which
step have
you reached
today?

I WON'T DO IT.

I CAN'T DO IT.

I WANT TO DO IT.

HOW DO I DO IT?

I'LL TRY TO DO IT.

I CAN DO IT.

I WILL DO IT.

YES, I DID IT!

Beautiful Oops

Materials

A *Beautiful Oops* by Barney Saltzberg, a box labeled "Oops Box" with leftover scraps, colored crayons, scissors, glue (whatever materials you wish to use).

You can get inspired from the website:
Beautiful Oops Share Idea
http://www.beautifuloops.com/share-ideas/

Procedures

1. Ask students to think about a mistake that they have made in the past week. What mistakes have you made this year?

2. If you can't think of one, listen to these examples and give a thumbs up if you have done these things:

    Have you ever called your teacher, Mom?
    Have you ever answered a math question wrong in class?
    Have you ever forgotten homework at home?

3. We have all made mistakes before, and that is part of learning. Part of getting better at something (and messing up less often) comes with practicing a new skill. For example, you might make less mistakes in math if you practice. Some mistakes are just accidents, like spilling a drink, and those times, you have to just understand that accidents happen. In fact, some mistakes can be made into successes… some "oopses" can be beautiful.

4. Read *A Beautiful Oops* by Barney Saltzberg.

5. Have students at their seats and then bring out a box labeled "Oops Box". Tell students that the things in this OOPS BOX are actually trash/things to be recycled or thrown away. They are pieces of trash, mess ups and "Oopses".

6. Tell students, "Since we are learning about making mistakes into something beautiful, I am going to challenge you to make these throw away things into art work.

    Show students this video, starting from the 3:00 minute marker:
    Barney Saltzberg's Beautiful Oops, full video
    https://www.youtube.com/watch?v=B0A3QhGVyDs

7. Have students complete a creative art piece and display them as "Mistakes Can Be Beautiful".

The Power Of Yet
Everyone Can Learn to Ride a Bicycle

Materials

Everyone Can Learn to Ride a Bicycle by Chris Raschka, "Rubric for Do You Get It Yet?" (page 87), "Power of Yet Poem" (below and page 91), and videos:

Growth Mindset Video
https://www.youtube.com/watch?v=ElVUqv0v1EE

Sesame Street: Janelle Monae - Power of Yet
https://www.youtube.com/watch?v=XLeUvZvuvAs

Procedures

1. Look at "Rubric for Do You Get It Yet?" (page 87) and think about where you are in the journey of learning to ride a bicycle. If you are high up on the rubric, try and think of when you were learning.

2. Read the story, *Everyone Can Learn to Ride a Bicycle* by Chris Raschka.

3. Tell students that learning anything is in the trying. The not giving up even if you don't get it **YET**.

4. Split students into small groups of 2-4 students. Groups will have 10 minutes to practice the poem "Power of Yet" (below and page 91) and then perform it in front of the group without having the words.

POWER OF YET POEM By Lisa King

I can't do it, I don't get it
Maybe I should just forget it
People all around me say
To just stick with it day to day.
They say things like "Don't you fret,
You just don't get it YET."
YET you say, YET you teach
All things could be within my reach?

YES!
You mean I'll learn it eventually
I'll understand it mentally.
All in good time, the power's in waiting
While keeping up the grit and training.
Telling my brain that I will get
Growth Mindset and the Power of YET.

---

5. After ten minutes, allow groups to perform their rendition of this poem.

6. **Optional:** Use a director's clapboard to start each act. At the end, give out Academy Awards and allow the winner to make a speech.

7. After the performance, with all students back in their own chairs, process how some people could memorize this more quickly (but if you had "stayed on the bike" and practiced it over and over, eventually everyone would have gotten it.)

90

POWER OF YET POEM

By Lisa King

I can't do it, I don't get it

Maybe I should just forget it

People all around me say

To just stick with it day to day.

They say things like "Don't you fret,

You just don't get it **YET.**"

YET you say, **YET** you teach

All things could be within my reach?

YES!

You mean I'll learn it eventually

I'll understand it mentally.

All in good time, the power's in waiting

While keeping up the grit and training.

Telling my brain that I will get

Growth Mindset and the **Power of YET.**

Mindset Matters

Part TWO 2
Chapter 4

Determination and Grit

"Grit is living life like it's a marathon, not a sprint."
– Angela Lee Duckworth

Resources to Teach Determination and Grit

Bibliotherapy List

The following books are great resources to supplement the lessons in this chapter on the subject of determination and grit.

Grit & Bear It!
by MS Zentic

Samantha on a Roll
by Linda Ashman

Stuck
by Oliver Jeffers

The Race
by Caroline Repchuk

Wilma Unlimited
by Kathleen Krull

Winners Never Quit
by Mia Hamm

***Sally Jean
Bicycle Queen***
by Cari Best

Video Clips to Teach Determination and Grit

Determination and GRIT	URL	Length
Carol Dweck: The Effect of Praise on Mindsets	https://www.youtube.com/watch?v=TTXrV0_3UjY	3:25
TMB Panyee FC Short Film: Make the Difference	https://www.youtube.com/watch?v=jU4oA3kkAWU	5:18

continued on next page

How Many Times Should You Try Before Success?	https://www.youtube.com/watch?v=I10vxL0VJO0	1:55
Grit: The Key to Your Success at FLVS	https://www.youtube.com/watch?v=uwsZZ2rprqc&feature=youtu.be	2:22
Amazing Kids of Character: Perseverance (Accessible Preview)	https://www.youtube.com/watch?v=1WXL2peOPG4	4:08
Amazing Kids of Character: Portraits of Perseverance	https://www.youtube.com/watch?v=S7vouKO84oI	1:44
Don't Stop Don't Give Up	https://www.youtube.com/watch?v=7uUlOAyQsn4	1:18
Sesame Street: Bruno Mars: Don't Give Up	https://www.youtube.com/watch?v=pWp6kkz-pnQ	1:57
Warhawk Matt Scott in Nike 'No Excuses' Commercial	https://www.youtube.com/watch?v=obdd31Q9PqA	1:01
Will Smith Mindset	https://www.youtube.com/watch?v=IJKIgtCpwvg&list=PLfM-YfRNOOtoPuUcmpGa2avMI6Q0YtbUi&index=51	1:26

Name _____

Are You DETERMINED to Crack the Code?

Directions: Try to figure out the phrase below by cracking the code. This puzzle can be solved by figuring out what letter each number represents. For example, when you look at the first number 9, the key tells us that it represents the letter I. So, for each 9 write the letter "I" in the box above it. See how quickly you can figure out this phrase about determination. Remember, don't give up!

KEY:

A	B	C	D	E	F	G	H	I	J	K	L	M	N	O	P	Q	R	S	T	U	V	W	X	Y	Z
11	1	7	12	10	25	24	3	9	19	23	22	13	17	14	18	26	15	4	2	20	5	6	8	16	21

PUZZLE:

9 25

16 14 20

17 10

15 10 25 20 4 10

7 11 17

14 17 10

16 14 20

11 15 10

3 10 22 18

12 10 2 10 15 13 9 17 10

16 14 20

2 14

22 10 11 15 4

17 14

14 17 10

7 11 17

22 10 11 15 17

9 25

16 14 20

4 2 14 18

17 14

14 17 10

7 11 17

22 11 15 17

16 14 20

20 5 18

20 14 20

Pipe Cleaner Perseverance Challenge

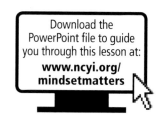

Download the PowerPoint file to guide you through this lesson at: **www.ncyi.org/ mindsetmatters**

Materials

10 pipe cleaners for each group of students, "Pipe Cleaner Perserverance Challenge Reflection Sheet" worksheet (page 99), gallon Ziploc bag, *GRIT and Bear It* by MS Zentic, ruler, download "MSM_PowerPoint 5" from website.

Procedures

1. Show PPT titled "MSM_PowerPoint 5" to help guide this lesson.

2. Divide students into teams of 3–5 people.

3. Distribute a gallon Ziploc bag filled with a bundle of 10 pipe cleaners, the "Pipe Cleaner Perserverance Challenge Reflection Sheet" worksheet (page 99), and a pencil to each team.

4. Tell students that this is a contest to see which team can build the "tallest structure" with the pipe cleaners in 7 minutes. The structure cannot be held or wedged between desks/ tables. If a team breaks the rules, a pipe cleaner will be taken away as a consequence.

5. After working for a few minutes tell students, "Freeze! I have just learned of a new challenge that has just been issued, and each team member must put one arm behind his/her back."

6. After a few more minutes, tell the teams that they can now use both arms, but now they need to continue the task without any talking. (This helps with chaos level as well).

7. Remind students when there is one minute left.

8. After you call, "Times up!" tell the class that before you decide who won, teams can earn bonus points by answering the questions with their team on the Reflection Sheet on page 99.

9. Measure with the ruler the tallest structure and add bonus points.

10. Talk about the qualities that often lead to success. Explain the definitions of grit and determination.

11. Read the book, *GRIT and Bear It*. Review what does grit means with video:
Don't Stop, Don't Give Up
https://www.youtube.com/watch?v=7uUlOAyQsn4

Extension Ideas

Distribute "How Gritty are You?" worksheet (page 101). Review with students to see if their answers match their behavior from this activity.

After this lesson, send the sample email to teachers (page 108).

Pipe Cleaner Perseverance Challenge Reflection Sheet

Directions

Everyone in the group should think about these questions.

1. List two character traits necessary to be successful at this activity.

2. In your group, vote to see which you liked better:

   a. trying to win
   -or-
   b. the challenge of the activity?

   • How many voted **a**?

   • How many voted **b**?

3. What does determination mean?

-- ✂ -----

Pipe Cleaner Perseverance Challenge Reflection Sheet

Directions

Everyone in the group should think about these questions.

1. List two character traits necessary to be successful at this activity.

2. In your group, vote to see which you liked better:

   a. trying to win
   -or-
   b. the challenge of the activity?

   • How many voted **a**?

   • How many voted **b**?

3. What does determination mean?

How Gritty are You?

Materials

Sally Jean Bicycle Queen by Cari Best, 2 balls, "How Gritty Are You?" worksheet (page 101),

Optional: 2 Plush Neurons (available on amazon.com)

Procedures

1. Ask for 4 student volunteers. Have each student stand facing a partner about 5 steps apart.

2. Give each pair one ball.

3. Have one pair of students throw a ball back and forth. Each time they catch it, they step forward until they are so close that they can hand the ball to each other.

4. Have the other pair throw their ball back and forth one time stepping forward when they catch it, and then freeze.

5. Explain that the two students who threw the ball back and forth and are now standing toe to toe can literally do this with their eyes closed.

6. Explain that just like when you tossed the ball, you looked for your partner to put out their hands and send a signal of readiness. In the same way, your brain cells have their arms reaching out when you are learning a skill. The distance represents the connection (literally the synapse).

7. Review that you see the pair who did a skill once and stopped still have a hard time doing it. But when we do a skill over and over, our neurons move closer and the connection is so easy that we can literally do it with our eyes closed.

8. Distribute the "How Gritty Are You?" worksheet (page 101).

9. Have students complete the survey and add up their score.

10. Explain what grit is.

11. Review the ball throwing activity. When you practice a skill, it becomes easier because your brain hardly has to think about it (it can do the skill without hardly trying). Use the plush neurons as visuals as to what is going on in our brain.

12. Read *Sally Jean Bicycle Queen*, and discuss grit.

13. Review with the students that their teacher can point out in this class students that have grit. Not students who make A's every time. Although these "A" students could indeed be gritty. But sometimes, there are students that have grit and determination to not give up **EVEN** if they are not an "A" student.

Name _____ Date_____

How Gritty are You?

Directions

Circle the answer that best describes you of 1-5 according to the descriptions above the numbers. Remember there are no right or wrong answers.

	Strongly Agree	Agree	Not Sure/ Sometimes	Disagree	Strongly Disagree
1. I have been able to work through some hard times.	5	4	3	2	1
2. I am embarrassed to ask my teacher for help when I need it.	5	4	3	2	1
3. I am very focused on getting my work done.	5	4	3	2	1
4. When things don't go my way, I keep on working and don't let it get me down.	5	4	3	2	1
5. I can stay focused, even when something is boring.	5	4	3	2	1
6. I am a hard-working person.	5	4	3	2	1
7. I have many activities that I'm really interested in.	5	4	3	2	1
8. Long assignments are difficult for me.	5	4	3	2	1
9. I always finish what I start.	5	4	3	2	1
10. Even when classwork is difficult, I work at it until I get it done.	5	4	3	2	1

Now, write the number that you circled for the following questions:

Question 1 _____
Question 3 _____
Question 4 _____
Question 6 _____
Question 9 _____
Question 10 _____

Total when I add the underlined numbers = _____

Adapted from the 12 point GRIT scale: Duckworth, A.L., Peterson, C., Matthews, M.D., & Kelly, D.R. (2007). Grit: Perseverance and passion for long-term goals. Journal of Personality and Social Psychology, 9, 1087-1101.

See below for a scale of how GRITTY you are:

30-28
You are the grittiest of the gritty.

27-25
You definitely have grit, lots of it.

24-20
You try and keep trying.

19-13
Most of the time, you give your best effort.

12-6
You need to focus a bit more on trying your best.

Give it your best

Redo when needed

Ignore giving up

Take your time

Winners Never Quit:
Goal Setting

Materials

Winners Never Quit by Mia Hamm, "Choose Which Word" worksheet (page 104) or "Set Your Goals" worksheet (page 106), and video:

The Wall: TV Commercial
www.values.com/inspirational-stories-tv-spots/85-The-Wall

1. Read *Winners Never Quit* by Mia Hamm.

2. Ask students, "What are some characteristics that Mia shows in this book?"

3. Ask students to think of as many words as possible that mean the same thing as determination.

> **Related Words Include:**
> - Persistence
> - Perseverance
> - Stamina
> - Hard Work
> - Grit
> - Tenacity
> - With Purpose

4. Review the analogy of reaching a goal being similar to that of climbing a ladder to reach a goal with the reward at the top of the ladder. Discuss how others might try to "shake the ladder" trying to make you fall. Others support you by "holding the ladder steady".

5. Watch this video clip on hard work:
The Wall: TV Commercial
www.values.com/inspirational-stories-tv-spots/85-The-Wall

6. Distribute either "Choose Which Word" worksheet (page 104) or "Set Your Goals" worksheet (page 106) to reinforce the concepts in this lesson.

Name _____ Date_____

Choose which word you think describes you.

Directions

From the word list, choose one of these words to write below the phrase "I HAVE."
Afterwards, draw a picture of yourself showing that character trait in the empty space.

WORD LIST: Grit, Determination, Perseverance, Stamina, Endurance, Persistence

Name _____ Date_____

Persistence PUZZLE

Directions

You have 5 minutes to complete this puzzle. Remember to work hard, show determination, and don't give up.

```
R  H  Z  U  D  T  J  X  C  H  N  T  T  C  Y
V  H  A  G  K  F  G  H  W  H  O  T  I  E  A
M  W  N  R  U  Y  Q  I  G  B  I  E  C  R  Z
G  P  T  O  D  O  X  S  P  C  T  N  B  L  G
E  C  F  Q  V  W  T  U  M  Y  A  A  Q  F  W
G  R  O  S  G  A  O  I  Y  R  N  C  V  H  C
E  W  K  N  M  Y  T  R  E  N  I  I  J  F  P
Y  C  X  I  X  I  R  V  K  R  M  T  P  J  F
E  Y  N  J  P  H  E  B  O  O  R  Y  B  G  Z
P  A  F  E  K  S  X  N  M  S  E  O  H  Q  H
E  S  O  P  R  U  P  V  Q  A  T  V  E  U  F
L  Y  Z  E  Q  U  Q  W  E  R  E  M  F  R  T
Z  W  P  U  Q  X  Q  X  B  O  D  A  U  M  F
P  E  R  S  I  S  T  E  N  C  E  P  U  T  T
Y  A  H  R  Y  C  E  G  A  U  R  B  T  H  F
```

DETERMINATION   **GRIT**   **HARDWORK**
PERSEVERANCE   **PERSISTENCE**   **PURPOSE**
STAMINA   **TENACITY**

Name _____ Date_____

Set Your Goals!
You Have the GRIT To Do It!

Directions

Answer the three questions in the soccer ball. Then write some of your favorite quotes about determination and grit in the ball.

What is a goal I have for when I'm grown up?

What is a goal for home?

What is a one of my goals in school?

GOALS

Quotes About Determination and GRIT

All right Mister, let me tell you what winning means... you're willing to go longer, work harder.

— Vincent Lombardi

Continuous effort–not strength or intelligence–is the key to unlocking our potential.

— Winston S. Churchill

A dream doesn't become reality through magic; it takes sweat, determination and hard work.

— Colin Powell

It's not that I'm smart, it's just that I stay with problems longer.

— Albert Einstein

Success is the sum of small efforts, repeated day in and day out.

— Robert Collier

Sample Email to Teachers

Here is an example of an email that would be a great follow up to a lesson on **Determination** and **Grit**.

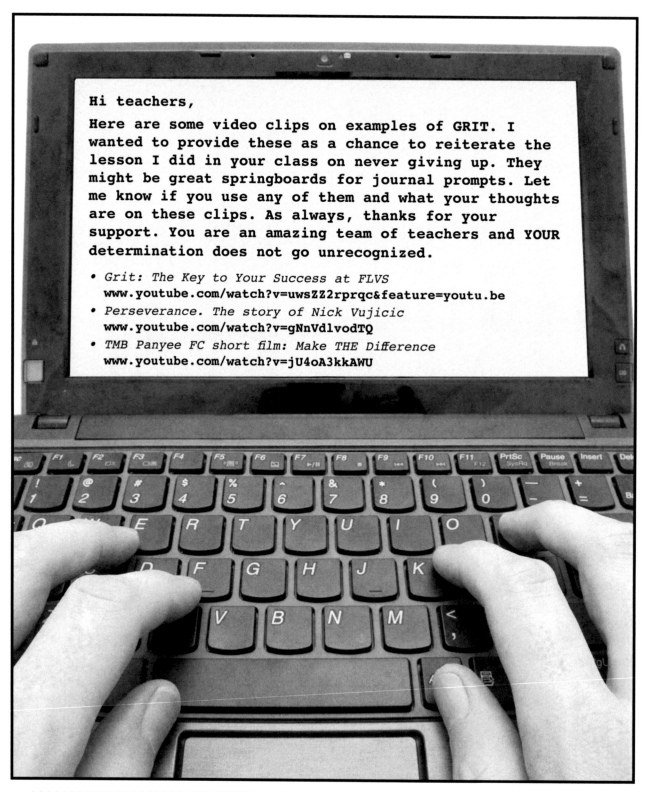

Hi teachers,

Here are some video clips on examples of GRIT. I wanted to provide these as a chance to reiterate the lesson I did in your class on never giving up. They might be great springboards for journal prompts. Let me know if you use any of them and what your thoughts are on these clips. As always, thanks for your support. You are an amazing team of teachers and YOUR determination does not go unrecognized.

- Grit: The Key to Your Success at FLVS
  www.youtube.com/watch?v=uwsZZ2rprqc&feature=youtu.be
- Perseverance. The story of Nick Vujicic
  www.youtube.com/watch?v=gNnVdlvodTQ
- TMB Panyee FC short film: Make THE Difference
  www.youtube.com/watch?v=jU4oA3kkAWU

Name _____ Date_____

Determination Interview

PART 1

Directions

Think about someone you know who is a hard worker. This should be a person that has worked hard to accomplish their goals. This person might have had challenges in their life and overcome these challenges.

Write the name of the person you are interviewing:

_____

How do you know this person?

_____

_____

PART 2

Directions

Ask the person you are interviewing the following questions:

What are 2 things you have done in your life that have taken lots of determination and hard work?

1. _____

2. _____

What advice would you give about sticking with it to accomplish a goal?

_____

_____

How do you show determination in your life each day?

_____

_____

_____

Signature of Person Interviewed

. . . .

What To Do When You Feel STUCK?

Materials

Stuck by Oliver Jeffers. "How to Solve a Problem" worksheet (page 111)

Procedures

1. Ask students if they have ever had a problem? (Students will answer anything from friendship problems to having arguments in the family, to not understanding school work, etc.)

2. Talk about different ways of solving problems. One way (that doesn't often work) is throwing solutions at problems ("Throwing everything plus the kitchen sink!") simply doesn't always work.

3. Explain that the saying "throwing the kitchen sink at it" means trying anything at all without necessarily thinking it through.

4. We will talk about solving it the SMART way in a moment, but for now, let me read you a story.

5. Read *Stuck* by Oliver Jeffers.

6. Discuss character traits the boy showed to solve the problem. These characteristics are necessary no matter how you choose to solve the problem,

7. Instead of "throwing the kitchen sink" (literally) at the problem, you could look at solving the problem by setting up a SMART goal.

8. Distribute worksheet "How to Solve a Problem" (page 111) to groups of 2-3 students.

9. Sample problems that could be used are:

   • I have a big Social Studies test next week, and I am so nervous.

   • My best friend is now friends with the new student at school, and I feel left out.

   • My brother and I are always fighting over what TV show to watch.

   • I really want to buy a gift for my mom's birthday, but I need extra money.

Extension Ideas:

   • If you were the boy in the story *Stuck*, what would your SMART GOAL have been?

   • Watch this video: *Amazing Kids of Character: Portraits of Perseverance*
     www.youtube.com/watch?v=S7vouKO84oI

Name _____ Date_____

How to Solve a Problem

What is the problem?

What SIZE problem is this?

☐ small

☐ Medium

☐ **LARGE**

What characteristics will you need to solve the problem?

_____

_____

_____

_____

_____

_____

_____

_____

_____

Sometimes, instead of throwing the kitchen sink at the problem: stop, and plan to solve the problem using a SMART plan. If it doesn't work, change up your goal and your method. For the problem you chose above, explain how your plan is:

Specific _____

_____

_____

Measurable _____

_____

Achievable _____

_____

Results-focused_____

_____

_____

Time-based _____

_____

_____

Mindset Matters

Part **TWO** *2*

Chapter 5

Self-Talk

If you think you are happy you are right.
If you think you are unhappy you are right.
– Author Unknown

Resources for Teaching Self-Talk
Bibliotherapy List

The following books are great resources to supplement the lessons in this chapter on the subject of positive self-talk.

 **Tiger, Tiger Is It True?** by Byron Katie and Hans Wilheim

 Sergio Makes a Splash by Edel Rodriguez

 **No Biggy** by Elycia Rubin

 Good News, Bad News by Jeff Mack

 Carla's Sandwich by Debbie Herman

 Some Dogs Do by Jez Alborough

 **Bounce Back! A Book About Resilience** by Cheri J. Meiners M.Ed

 **A.N.T. Annoying Nonsense Thoughts: A Guide to Positive Thinking** by Sara Parker

 **A Happy Hat** by Cecil Kim

 Rain Brings Frogs by MaryAnn Cocca-Leffler

 Don't Feed the Monster on Tuesday by Adolph Moser

 The Worst Day of My Life... EVER! by Julia Cook

 **It's Tough to Lose Your Balloon** by Jarrett J. Krosoczka

 **One of Those Days** by Amy Krouse Rosenthal

 **The Dot** by Peter Reynolds

Video Clips to Teach Self-Talk

Self-Talk	URL	Length
Jessica's "Daily Affirmation"	https://www.youtube.com/watch?v=qR3rK0kZFkg	:49
Do or Do not there is no try - Yoda Star Wars: The Empire Strikes Back	https://www.youtube.com/watch?v=eExL1VLkQYk	1:00
Teaching Positive Thinking	https://www.youtube.com/watch/?v=SQIVslZIMXI	0:49
Positive & Negative Thinking Great Lesson	https://www.youtube.com/watch?v=B-qJ8fu0rrI	2:00
Power of Positive Thinking	https://www.youtube.com/watch?v=NL1JEn3ahx8	1:17
Crabby Little Girl–Clip	https://www.youtube.com/watch?v=TkGLRhHipUk	1:41
Finding Nemo - Just Keep Swimming.flv	https://www.youtube.com/watch/?v=hbgD-r-tYzQ	:30

Positive Thinking = Growth Mindset

Download the PowerPoint file to guide you through this lesson at:
www.ncyi.org/ mindsetmatters

Materials

Download "MSM_PowerPoint 6," "Brain Riddles" (page 70), "Mindset Chant" (page 13), "Positive Thinking = Growth Mindset" worksheet (page 119), and video:

Positive & Negative Thinking Great Lesson
https://www.youtube.com/watch?v=B-qJ8fu0rrI

Procedures

1. This lesson follows the PPT titled "MSM_PowerPoint 6."

2. Begin the lesson with "Brain Riddles" (page 70). Allow students to guess answers.

3. Tell students that we use our brains in many ways: to solve puzzles, to learn, and in choosing how we behave. The thoughts we have determine our attitudes.

4. Do the "Mindset Chant" (page 13) with students. Discuss that staying positive is a skill that comes more naturally to some people, and that other people have to train their brains to stay positive.

5. Discuss different sayings that mean "stay positive" (i.e.: Look on the bright side, when life gives you lemons make lemonade, etc.)

6. Positive thinking or positive self-talk is a big part of growth mindset.

7. Review samples of ways to change your words ➔ to change your mindset.

8. Distribute "Positive Thinking = Growth Mindset" worksheet (page 119).

Change Your Words
Change Your Mindset

I give up! → I'm going have to use what I know to try this.

I messed up on this. → Mistakes will help me learn.

I'm not as good as they are at this. → I'm going to try and use some of the same ways they are doing this to see if it works for me.

This will never get better. → If I train my brain to think positively, things will improve.

Positive Thinking = Growth Mindset

😞 INSTEAD OF THINKING	😊 TRY THINKING
1. Nobody wants to play with me at recess.	
2. My parents are so mean. They make me go to bed so early.	
3. I did awful on that test. I am so bad at Math.	
4. My soccer team lost the championship game. We stink.	
5. I can't believe I wasn't invited to that birthday party.	

Carla's Sandwich:
Finding the Positive in YOU

Materials

Carla's Sandwich by Debbie Herman, "Positive Thinking Sandwich" worksheet (page 121)

Procedures

1. Read the story, *Carla's Sandwich* by Debbie Herman (I find this especially appropriate to read during lunch bunch since it is all about sandwiches.)

2. Discuss how Carla was confident about things that made her different. Ask what does confident mean? Discuss how being confident helps us to feel positive.

3. Have students stand in a circle, and tell them we need to appreciate what makes us special and different. We need to be proud/confident of these qualities.

4. Ask students to step into the middle of the circle if:

- You are a student at this school
- You like chocolate
- You have any brothers
- You have been at this school since kindergarten
- You like PE
- You are good at Math
- You are a good singer
- You are a fast runner
- You are a good friend
- You can name one quality about yourself that you like. Can you think of two? Three?

5. Distribute "Positive Thinking Sandwich" worksheet (page 121).

6. Tell students that they will now work in pairs to come up with positive things about themselves.

7. Students can work in pairs to fill in the positive qualities to make up their "sandwich" using outer traits where the outer part of the sandwich is (the 2 pieces of bread) and positive inner qualities where the inside parts of the sandwich are.

8. After completing this, ask students to share with the larger group.

Positive Thinking Sandwich

Being Positive on the Inside and Outside

What Positive Things Can You Think About Yourself?

Name _____   Name _____

Positive Attitude Helps Positive Self-Esteem

The Dot:
Confidence vs. Competence

Materials

The Dot by Peter Reynolds (story available online at Tumblebooks.com), "Confidence Competence" worksheet (page 123)

Procedures

1. Introduce the terms confidence vs. competence using "Confidence Competence" worksheet (page 123). You can hand out copies or display on a screen.

   • **Confidence** - *believing* I can do something.

   • **Competence** - *being able* to do something well.

2. Talk about the importance of having confidence and competence. Discuss ways to improve feelings of confidence as learners.

3. Introduce *The Dot* story as an example of seeing someone's confidence in a skill improve. Encourage students to be attentive to the story to figure out what made the girl's confidence improve.

4. Have students discuss how the main character's confidence improved in the beginning, middle and end of the story.

5. Students can complete the information section of the "Confidence Competence" worksheet (page 123) independently by writing the definitions for confidence and competence based on what they learned from the lesson.

Extension

Watch the video of the song that goes with this book:
The Bouncing Dot Music Video
www.fablevisionlearning.com/blog/2014/08/the-dot-song

122

Term	Definition	Picture
Confidence		
Competence		

Positive Problem Solving

Download the
PowerPoint file to guide
you through this lesson at:
**www.ncyi.org/
mindsetmatters**

Materials

Small amount of Activity Dough and small rock for each student. Put both in a small, snack-sized sealable sandwich bag. Download "MSM_ PowerPoint 6," "Mindset Chant" mini poster (page 13), "Positive Problem Solving" worksheet (page 125) , "Postive Thinking = Growth Mindset" mini poster (page 126)

Procedures

To prepare for this lesson, you will need to fill sandwich bags (one per student) with a small amount of Activity Dough and a small rock. Bring a basket or bag filled with all of these sandwich bags to the class or group. This lesson follows the PPT titled, "MSM_PowerPoint 6."

1. Tell students, "Think a minute about the last few days, at home, with your friends, at school. Raise your hand if you can think of a problem you faced, big or little." Take some examples from students.

2. Distribute baggie of Activity Dough and a rock to each student.

3. Give students these instructions one at a time:

   • Take out your Activity Dough. Change it into something else. Were you able to change it?

   • Take out your rock. Change it into something else. Were you able to change it?

4. Describe to the students that there are two types of problems: Activity Dough problems that you can control and rock problems that you cannot control.

5. Give examples of each: What type of problem is it when you call out? (Activity Dough problem) What kind of problem is a soccer game getting rained out? (rock problem).

6. Discuss that regardless of what type of problem we have, it can always be made better with positive self-talk. What is another name for positive thinking? (Looking on the bright side, When life gives you lemons make lemonade, OR Having a Growth Mindset!)

7. Have students stand up and learn/review "Mindset Chant" (page 13) and discuss that sometimes the skill you are working on is being positive. You can train your brain to do this, but it might not be easy.

8. Discuss that having positive thinking is a skill we all have to work on.

9. Have students choose a partner for the next activity, "Using Positive Problem Solving" worksheet (page 125). In this activity, they will be challenged to think on the bright side when facing a problem.

10. Show "Postive Thinking = Growth Mindset" mini poster (page 126) as examples of Growth Mindset statements that can be used to show positive thinking.

11. Discuss how it is important when trying to solve a problem to know whether it is a rock problem or an Activity Dough problem.

124

Positive Problem Solving

STEP 1: Choose a problem from the choices below and circle it.

PROBLEM 1 You failed a math test.	**PROBLEM 2** You didn't clean your room, so you can't go outside and play.	**PROBLEM 3** You got into a fight with your friend and called him/her a loser.
PROBLEM 4 Your dad has the flu and can't take you to the movies.	**PROBLEM 5** You didn't get invited to a classmate's birthday party.	**PROBLEM 6** You get a gift from your aunt that you don't like.

STEP 2: Is this is a **Rock Problem** or an **Activity Dough Problem**? (circle what you think).

Rock Problem

You cannot change this. You have **NO** control.

Activity Dough Problem

You may be able to change this. You have some control.

STEP 3: What positive thought could you use to help look on the bright side of this problem?

_____

_____

_____

_____

_____

Postive Thinking = Growth Mindset

Examples of Growth Mindset (Positive Thinking) Statements

If I focus, I can do anything I set my mind to.

This gives me an opportunity to try something new.

Mistakes are part of learning; I'll just do my best.

I am disappointed, but I have other things I will focus on.

I can train my brain and with practice I WILL get it.

Seeing the Rainbow in the Rainstorm

Materials

One of the following books: *It's Tough to Lose Your Balloon* by Jarrett J. Krosoczka, *Rain Brings Frogs* by MaryAnn Cocca-Leffler, or *One of Those Days* by Amy Krouse Rosenthal.

Balloons or bean bags (2 of any kind and one with "POSITIVE THINKING" written on it.), "Negative Thinking/Fixed Mindset Statement Cards" (page 130), "Seeing the Rainbow in the Rainstorm" worksheet (page 131)

Procedures

1. Read a story about looking on the bright side of things (such as *It's Tough to Lose Your Balloon, Frogs Bring Rain,* or *One of Those Days*).

2. After the story, ask for four volunteers. Have the students stand facing; each pair the same distance apart.

3. Give each pair a balloon (especially if you have just read *It's Tough to Lose your Balloon*) or a beanbag.

4. Have one pair throw the object back and forth. Each time they catch it, have them step forward until they are so close that they can hand the ball to each other.

5. Have the other pair throw a balloon (especially if you have just read *It's Tough to Lose your Balloon*) or a beanbag back and forth one time stepping forward when they catch it, and then freeze.

6. Explain that the two students who threw the ball back and forth and are now standing toe to toe can literally do this with their eyes closed.

7. Tell them that this is what happens with your brain cells as you learn a skill. The distance represents the connection (literally the synapse). You see the pair who did a skill once and stopped have a harder time doing it. But when you do a skill over and over, your neurons move closer and the connection is so easy that you can literally do it with your eyes closed.

continued on next page

8. For the students who are standing close to each other, take their balloon/beanbag and hand them a new one with "POSITIVE THINKING" written on it. Tell students that positive thinking is a skill that is natural for some. Others need to train their brains.

9. Distribute "Seeing the Rainbow in the Rainstorm" worksheet (page 131) to students. Tell them that we will be working on changing negative thoughts to positive thoughts. We need to train our brains to this type of thinking.

10. Review the process:

- Negative Thought: I will never understand multiplication!!

- Positive Thought: If I keep trying, I know I will do better at multiplication.

> **Differentiation:** If you want to provide your students with a choice of activities to scaffold the level of difficulty, the coloring sheet on page 129 can take the place of the activity described in Procedures 9 through 11.

11. Distribute "Negative Thinking/Fixed Mindset Statement Cards" (page 130) to each student or pair of students if they are working together. These cards will be used on the "Seeing the Rainbow in the Rainstorm" worksheet (page 131).

Extension

Counselor can tell students an example of a negative thought, and the students can write on a sticky note an idea of how to change it to a positive thought. The student with the best idea will be recorded on the audio app on the IPad. (They love to hear their voices).

© National Center For Youth Issues • www.ncyi.org • 866-318-6294
Please refer to page 2 for duplication information

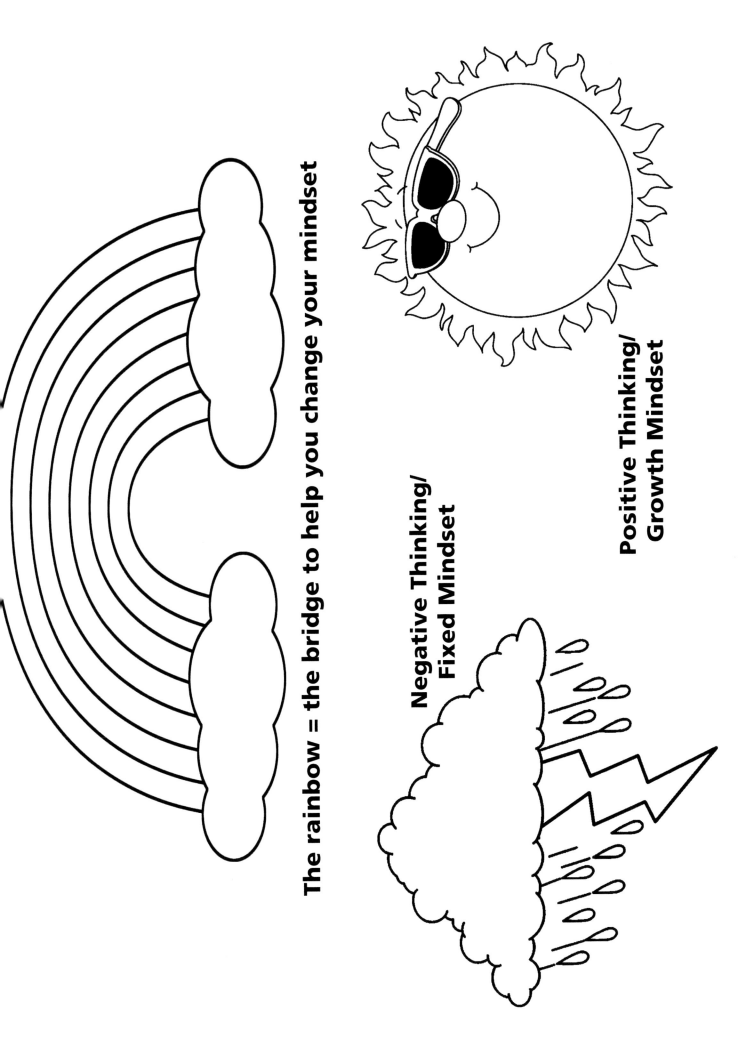

The rainbow = the bridge to help you change your mindset

**Negative Thinking/
Fixed Mindset**

**Positive Thinking/
Growth Mindset**

Seeing the Rainbow in the Rainstorm

Name _____ Date _____

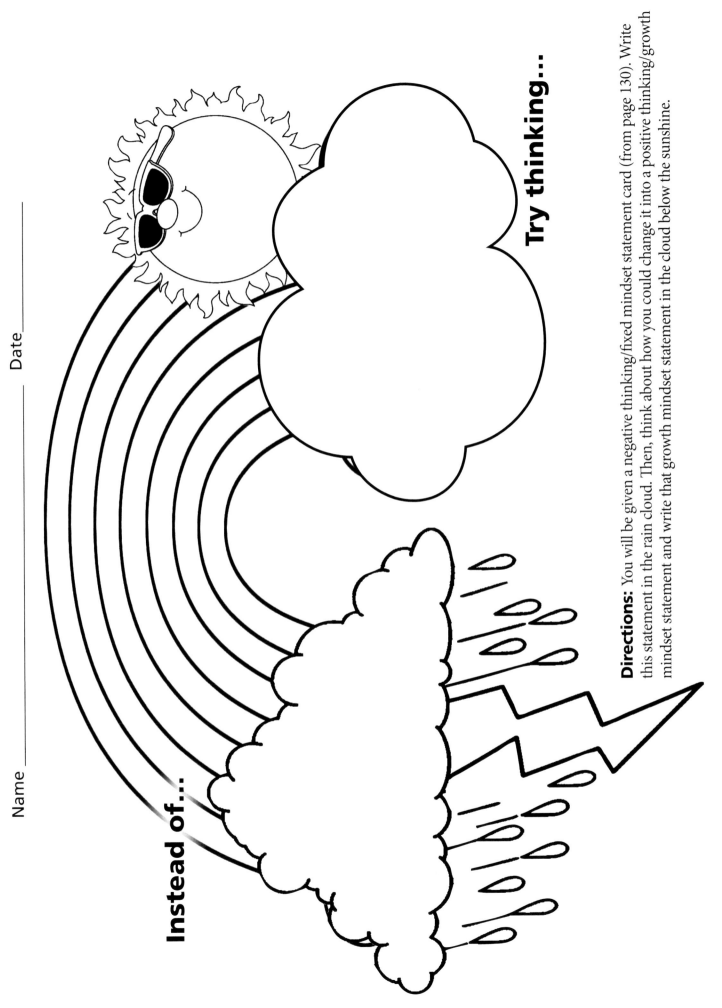

Instead of...

Try thinking...

Directions: You will be given a negative thinking/fixed mindset statement card (from page 130). Write this statement in the rain cloud. Then, think about how you could change it into a positive thinking/growth mindset statement and write that growth mindset statement in the cloud below the sunshine.

A Super Ball and an Egg: Bounce Back and Smile

Materials

Large piece of butcher paper or newspaper with a target drawn on it, one or more super ball(s), one or more raw or soft boiled eggs.

Procedures

1. Put a large piece of butcher paper with a target drawn on it on the floor. Without explaining yet, ask for two volunteers. The first takes the super ball and throws it at the target, trying to get closest to the center. The second student drops the egg.

2. Ask, "When the super ball was dropped, what happened? (answers will be things like "It bounced back.")

3. Ask, "When the egg was dropped, what happened? (answers will be things like, "It splatted.")

4. Explain that these objects represent two very different types of people: negative/egg people and positive/super ball people. When negative people hit a "bump in the road," they don't do well, usually giving up on their goal. When positive people hit an obstacle, they bounce back.

5. Have students work in groups of 3-5 kids.

6. Have each group create a song, poem/chant/rap about what it means to be a positive-thinking person.

Above lesson adapted from lesson
http://www.dol.gov/odep/topics/youth/softskills/Enthusiasm.pdf.

Optional Extension:

- For younger grades, you can read *Bounce Back! A Book About Resilience* by Cheri J. Meiners, M.Ed.

- Hand out bouncy balls to the class/group.

- Make copies of the cutout (right) and glue to the bottom of plastic cups for the kids to store them in.

- At the end of the project, you can send the "Super Ball and Egg" (page 133) letter home with students.

Bounce Back and Smile

Date:

Bounce Back and Smile

Dear Parents,

Your child is coming home with a Super Ball. This ball represents the lesson we just did on positive thinking, resiliency, and bouncing back. The lesson focused on turning obstacles into opportunities. The plastic cup container is to remind your child what the Super Ball represents and also to help them keep track of it.

With hopes that this ball provides opportunities to bounce back and smile!

Your child's counselor,

Date:

Bounce Back and Smile

Dear Parents,

Your child is coming home with a Super Ball. This ball represents the lesson we just did on positive thinking, resiliency, and bouncing back. The lesson focused on turning obstacles into opportunities. The plastic cup container is to remind your child what the Super Ball represents and also to help them keep track of it.

With hopes that this ball provides opportunities to bounce back and smile!

Your child's counselor,

Tiger, Tiger is it True?

Materials

"Self-Talk Situation" cards (located below)

Tiger, Tiger Is It True by Byron Katie and Hans Wilheim. You may also watch a version of this book online: *Tiger Tiger Is It True?*
www.youtube.com/watch?v=gPfB4CR6fUU&index=1&list=RDgPfB4CR6fUUT

Procedures

1. Explain that in the book we will read, Tiger learns that what causes problems are usually our thoughts and feelings about what is going on. Typically, if your thoughts can be turned positive, problems magically seem smaller.

2. Teach students the process of situation → thoughts → feelings.

3. After reading the book, have students divide into groups.

4. Instruct groups that they will be given a situation from situation cards below. The groups have a choice of how to present it to the group. They can 1) act out the situation; or 2) describe the situation and how to turn it around with positive thinking. (Tell the students that if they act out the situation, the actor should say out loud what positive self-talk is going through his/her mind.)

Self-Talk Situation Cards

You don't have anyone to play with at recess.	You broke your leg and are on crutches, so you can't play on the playground during recess. You are getting tired of watching everyone have fun while you have to watch.
You just don't understand your Math assignment. You want to just give up.	You are invited to a party, and you really want to go. Unfortunately, you have nothing new to wear and you don't have enough money to buy a new outfit.
You always get in trouble when you and your little sister or brother argue about what TV show to watch.	You are making an art project for your mom's birthday, and you are disappointed when it doesn't come out how you expected.

This video consists of 1:52 minutes of positive statements with serene music:
Daily Affirmations - Short Positive Affirmations Quotes
https://www.youtube.com/watch?v=rOEqCGtHEwg&feature=share

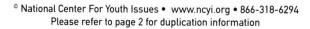

Mindset Matters

Part **TWO** 2
Chapter 6

Everyone Is Unique

Resources to Teach "Everyone is Unique"

We Are the Same, We Are Different

A Unique Word Search

Unique Signature Bingo

Only One You

Eggbert: It's What is on the Inside That Matters

Resources to Teach Everyone is Unique
Bibliotherapy List

The following books are great resources to supplement the lessons in this chapter on the subject of diversity and how everyone is unique.

Calvin Can't Fly
by Jennifer Berne

Hooray for You: A Celebration of You-Ness
by Marianne Richmond

Only One You
by Linda Kranz

Wink: The Ninja Who Wanted to be Noticed
by J.C. Phillipps

You Be You
by Linda Kranz

Beautiful, Beautiful Hair
by Melissa Parkington

Rosie's Story
by Martine Gogoll

Eggbert: The Slightly Cracked Egg
by Tom Ross

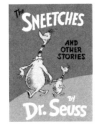

The Sneetches
by Dr. Seuss

Back to Front and Upside Down!
by Claire Alexander

It's OK to be Different
by Todd Parr

We are the Same, We are Different

Materials

It's Okay to be Different by Todd Parr or *Rosie's Story* by Martine Gogoll, for Choice 1: "Different Same Different" worksheet (page 139), For Choice 2: "We Are THE SAME in These Ways" worksheet (page 140) and "We Are DIFFERENT in These Ways" worksheet (page 141). Pencils and crayons; counselor will bind worksheets into a class book for choice 2 using "Same Different Class" (page 142) as the title page.

Procedures

1. Ask students to think about these questions, "Is there something that makes you different? Have you ever had the thought that you wanted to change something about yourself because it makes you different?"

2. Read *It's Okay to be Different* by Todd Parr or *Rosie's Story* by Martine Gogoll.

3. Discuss how at times we all feel uncomfortable with being different, but this is what makes us all unique.

4. Have students work in pairs on one of the two activities that follow. Choice 1 will be appropriate for a 30 minute lesson, while Choice 2 will take longer (lesson total will be about 45 minutes).

    a. Choice 1: Students can work in pairs on the "Different Same Different"worksheet (page 139) highlighting what the similarities and differences are between themselves and their partner.

    b. Choice 2: Students will work in pairs. In each pair, one student will get the "We Are THE SAME in these Ways" worksheet (page 140) and one will get the "We Are DIFFERENT in these Ways" worksheet (page 141). The two students will need to look at each other and talk to each other to discover differences and similarities that they have. Additionally, each student will do a portrait of their partner. Once the worksheets are complete, the counselor collects them and makes them into a class book.

Different   **Same**   **Different**

We are THE SAME
in these ways.

1. _____

2. _____

This is a picture of _____ .

We are DIFFERENT
in these ways.

1. _____

2. _____

This is a picture of
_____

WE ARE THE SAME, WE ARE DIFFERENT

BOOK ABOUT DIVERSITY

_____'S CLASS

Name _____ Date_____

A Unique Word Search

Directions

Directions: How many of these different words that mean *unique* can you find in the word search?

```
C  O  C  J  M  I  U  M  L  D  S  Y  Y  E  G
N  H  R  S  T  E  N  P  I  I  P  T  H  D  P
O  V  A  U  E  E  D  V  U  F  E  I  T  U  M
A  T  D  R  U  G  E  J  F  F  C  N  A  T  P
Y  R  Y  Q  A  R  R  V  V  E  I  U  P  I  Z
N  T  I  I  S  C  S  J  V  R  A  T  M  T  V
Z  N  I  I  Z  I  T  W  Y  E  L  R  E  T  X
U  X  T  V  X  Q  A  E  N  N  E  O  C  A  T
Q  Y  T  W  I  B  N  A  R  T  C  P  O  Z  H
T  R  U  S  T  T  D  D  Y  I  R  P  H  J  C
S  E  I  T  I  L  I  B  I  S  S  O  P  Y  L
A  U  V  X  S  Y  N  S  E  R  U  T  L  U  C
C  I  B  D  E  M  G  U  N  S  I  O  I  A  Y
A  C  C  E  P  T  A  N  C  E  C  E  S  C  M
U  K  S  H  T  G  N  E  R  T  S  M  C  L  S
```

ACCEPTANCE	ATTITUDE	CHARACTERISTICS
CULTURE	DIFFERENT	DIVERSITY
EMPATHY	OPPORTUNITY	POSSIBILITIES
SENSITIVITY	SPECIAL	STRENGTHS
TRUST	UNDERSTANDING	UNIQUE

© National Center For Youth Issues • www.ncyi.org • 866-318-6294
Please refer to page 2 for duplication information

Name _____ Date_____

Unique Signature Bingo

Directions

Try and find another person in the room that matches the description in the boxes below.

U	N	I	Q	U	E
I have more than 3 pets.	I have red hair.	I am good at Math.	I take piano lessons	I know how to speak 2 or more languages	My favorite color is purple.
I celebrate Hanukkah.	My birthday is in the summer.	I love to read.	I have gone to sleep-away summer camp.	I read every night.	I have always been a good friend.
I have run in a race before.	I think that I will go to college.	I actually like doing homework.	I have been snow skiing before.	I have on the same color as you.	I have blue eyes.
I know how to dive into the deep end of a swimming pool.	I have fallen while riding a bicycle before.	I have made a mistake today.	I celebrate Easter.	I often feel that I am different from other people.	When I am older, I think I will work very hard.
I am an only child.	I would rather play outside than play video games.	Social Studies is one of my favorite subjects.	I love learning about animals.	I have flown in an airplane.	I can name one activity that I am good at.
If I see someone playing alone, I try to include them.	I have played a certain sport for at least 3 years.	I am a good artist.	I think that being smart at computers is very cool.	I can count to 10 in Spanish.	I have won a competition before.

After playing this game I learned that I have this in common (the same) as another student in this group:

_____

_____

After playing this game I learned that I have this difference from one or more students in this group:

_____

_____

144

Only One You

Materials

Only One You or *You Be You* by Linda Kranz, "Only One Me" worksheet (page 147–markers/crayons, digital camera and printer will be needed for this activity) or "Fish Cut Out" worksheet (page 148), "Roll a Review Question" worksheet (page 146); several dice for review questions

Procedures

1. Start the lesson by showing the beautiful illustrations or "rockfish" in Linda Kranz's story *Only One You*. Each fish in her book is individually painted. Ask students what *unique* means.

2. Distribute "Only One Me" worksheet (page 147). Each student will uniquely color this underwater scene.

3. Read the story to the students while they are creating their underwater scene.

4. Explain to students that once the reading of the story is over, and as they finish their underwater scene (which will be UNIQUE timing for everyone), they can move to an area of the room designated for kids that are ready to answer discussion questions which will be done as noted on "Roll a Review Question" worksheet (page 146).

5. While students are involved in finishing the coloring and the review question activity, take a photo of each student standing in front of a blue background (piece of blue butcher paper taped onto the wall). Once these photos are printed, they can be glued to the rectangle.

Other alternative activities:

- Have each child draw a fish and display them on a bulletin board.

- Have each child make a thumbprint fish.

- Have each child make a paper plate fish by cutting away a triangle shape from one side of the paper plate to create the fish's mouth. Staple or glue the triangular piece you removed onto the side of the fish opposite the mouth to represent the fish's tail. Use the pencil and draw an eye, lips, and a fin on your fish. Fill in the areas of the fish with color using the markers. Everyone's fish will be different, and that's the point.

- Have each child make their own rockfish. They can either take this home, or a rock garden can be established where all of the rockfish are displayed.

Roll a Review Question

Directions

Students will work with one or two other students. Going one at a time, students roll the die and answer one of the questions in that box.

Name one unique quality about yourself.
– or –
How are the painted fish in the story unique?

Why is it important to respect each other's differences?
– or –
How can you make the world a better place?

What is something others might notice about you?
– or –
What is another word for unique?

Name 2 ways to make a new friend.
– or –
What are wise words you remember from this story?

How can a smile make someone's day better?
– or –
Name one thing that you have in common with all of your classmates.

Why is it a good thing that we are all different?
– or –
Smile at a friend and give them a compliment.

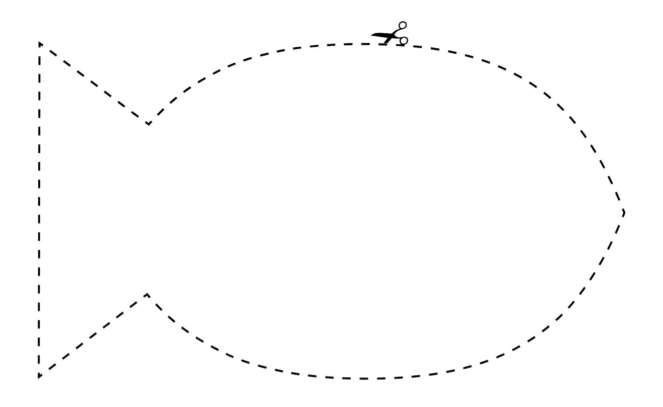

life is a grand journey
you be you

Eggbert: It's What's On The Inside that Matters

Materials

Eggbert: The Slightly Cracked Egg by Tim Ross, 1 brown egg, 1 white egg, 2 clear plastic cups.

Procedures:

1. Optional:
Show this trailer for *Eggbert: The Slightly Cracked Egg* to get students ready for this activity: *EGGBERT The Slightly Cracked Egg-EDM310 Kristen Phelps*
www.youtube.com/watch?v=H-MROaWNZFY

2. To introduce this lesson, show kids the two different eggs (white and brown) and ask if the kids think they could guess which one is which once they are cracked.

3. Turn around and crack each egg open in a separate plastic cup. Turn back around and have the students guess which one is which. Obviously, both look the same on the inside.

4. Discuss the danger of judging people only by the way they look.

5. Discuss how not only do we sometimes judge others for their differences, we also are hard on ourselves when we notice a flaw or "crack" in ourselves.

6. Read the book, *Eggbert: The Slightly Cracked Egg*, by Tim Ross.

7. Follow up with a discussion about how our differences make us unique, special, and that what we might see as flaws in ourselves can actually be beautiful.

Possible extensions

- Talk about how we need to accept our flaws and faults. Sometimes we need to have "thick skin." Use an eggshell to demonstrate its strength. Optionally have students make a shield or cover to give it "thick skin" and do an egg drop.

- Put Questions to story in plastic eggs.

- Do an egg-related craft (many ideas can be found online.)

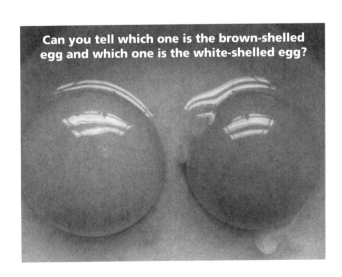

Can you tell which one is the brown-shelled egg and which one is the white-shelled egg?

Mindset
Matters

Part **TWO** 2

Chapter 7

Teach Others
What You Know

Why Teach to Others?

At the end of the *Mindset Matters* Curriculum (whether in group or classroom lessons), it is important to have students share what they have learned. We know that if students can teach what they know, it is a sign of mastery.

Tell students, "Now that you know about growth mindset we need your help. Scientists have discovered new things about the brain, and they want us to share these messages about success with you, so you in turn will tell your peers. These messages will mean a lot more coming from you than they will coming from adults like us."

There are many options in having the students teach what they have learned. Here are two ideas:

1. Make Posters Indicating what they learned:

Procedures

- Separate students into 7 groups (students in each group will depend on how many in the group or class.)

- Assign each group one of the letters in **MINDSET**. Have them create a poster about what they learned.

2. Choreographing the Mindset Chant

Procedures

- Students should get into groups of 3-5 students.

- Give copies of the "Mindset Chant" (page 13) to students. Have each group choreograph a way to present the mindset chant to the larger group.

Mindset Matters
End of Group Letter

Parents/Guardians,

This week is our last meeting for our Mindset Matters group. I wanted to let you know some of the things that we have been learning so that you can discuss these ideas with your child. The overriding theme throughout this group is to understand that your brain can grow if you work hard to practice a skill (for both academic and/or behavioral skills). We have broken down the idea of Growth Mindset by looking at each letter in the word MINDSET. Ask your child what they remember about each of the following ideas:

Mindfulness

Identifying Brain Basics

Not Yet is OK
(understanding you might not understand things right away)

Determination and Grit

Self-Talk and Positive Thinking

Everyone is Unique
(we all learn at a different pace)

Teach others what you learned (that's what your child is doing if they are reviewing this with you)

I look forward to seeing each of the students using their skills, and I hope that they enjoyed this group as much as I did. Please feel free to call me if you have any questions or feedback on how I can further support your child.

Sincerely,

Ms.King, School Counselor
678-494-7603 x231
lisa.king@cobbk12.org

Name _____ Class_____

Adult Signature _____

Growth Mindset Tic-Tac-Toe

For more information on Growth Mindset, watch this video clip:
Carol Dweck, 'Developing a Growth Mindset
https://www.youtube.com/watch?v=hiiEeMN7vbQ

Once you have completed 3 activities in a row, check them off for tic-tac-toe you! Then, bring this paper back to school and turn it into your counselor to be entered in a drawing for a prize.

Discuss with someone at home a new hobby you want to try.	**Draw a picture of yourself trying something new.**	**Think of a problem you had today and how you learned from this situation.**
Do the Growth Mindset Chant for someone at home.	**Say this out loud (so someone else can hear) "If I train my brain and practice a skill, I can do anything!"**	**Make up a poem about having determination and not giving up.**
Make JELLO with someone at home. (This is the consistency of the brain. Eeeew!)	**Talk about someone you admire who shows determination.**	**Start a jigsaw puzzle and set a goal for when you can complete it.**

© National Center For Youth Issues • www.ncyi.org • 866-318-6294
Please refer to page 2 for duplication information

Create a Door Hanger

Materials

Door hanger for each student (wooden or foam), copies of the "Mindset Chant" (below)

Procedures

1. Get door hangers (either foam or wooden) for each student.

2. Cut out the "Mindset Chant" (below) and make copies for each student.

3. Students can glue this to one side of the door hanger and decorate the other side as they wish.

MINDSET CHANT!

Whatcha gotta do?

I've got to train my brain.

Why you gotta do it?

Gotta show the world.

Whatcha gonna show them?

That I've got some skills.

What kind of skills?

Whatever I work on!

What's that called?

Growth Mindset, Growth Mindset,
Growth Mindset!

Go on a "Teach Others Walk-About"

Procedures

1. Make these question cards into necklaces and have students wear these as you walk around school.

2. Find adults along the way for students to approach, and the adults will read these tags and ask them questions.

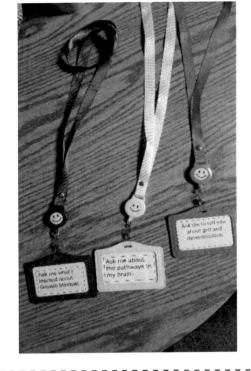

---✂--

> **Ask me to do the Mindset Chant.**

> **Ask me what I learned about Growth Mindset.**

> **Ask me about the pathways in my brain.**

> **Ask me to tell you about grit and determination.**

> **Ask me about why taking deep breaths is important.**

> **Ask me what it means to look on the bright side of things.**

> **Ask me why it is important to practice different skills.**

Mindset Matters

Part **THREE** 3

Appendix

Condensed Bibliotherapy List

Mindfulness

What Does It Mean to Be Present? by Rana DiOrio

A Handful of Quiet: Happiness in Four Pebbles by Thich Nhat Hanh

Mindful Monkey Happy Panda by Lauren Alderfer

Moody Cow Meditates by Kerryi Lee MacLean

Peaceful Piggy Meditation by Kerry Lee MacLean and Kerry MacLean

Silence by Lemniscates

Sitting Still Like a Frog by Eline Snel

You are a Lion by Taeeun Yoo

Identify Brain Basics

Your Fantastic Elastic Brain by Joann Deak

A Walk in the Rain with a Brain by Edward Hallowell and Bill Mayer

Think, Think, Think: Learning About Your Brain by Pamela Hill Nettleton

Young Genius: Brains by Kate Lennard

Not Yet is OK

Everyone Can Learn to Ride a Bicycle by Chris Raschka

Leo the Late Bloomer by Robert Kraus

Thanks for the Feedback (I Think) by Julia Cook

Beautiful Oops by Barney Salzberg

Emily's Art by Peter Catalanotto

Sergio Makes a Splash by Edel Rodriguez

I Will Never Not Ever Eat a Tomato by Lauren Child

The OK Book by Amy Krouse Rosenenthal and Tom Lichtenheld

Rosie Sprout's Time to Shine by Allison Wortche

Determination and Grit

Grit & Bear It! by MS Zentic

Stuck by Oliver Jeffers

Wilma Unlimited by Kathleen Krull

Samantha on a Roll by Linda Ashman

Winners Never Quit by Mia Hamm

Sally Jean Bicycle Queen by Cari Best

The Race by Caroline Repchuk

Self-Talk

Tiger, Tiger Is It True? by Byron Katie and Hans Wilheim

No Biggy by Elycia Rubin

Carla's Sandwich by Debbie Herman

A Happy Hat by Cecil Kim

Don't Feed the Monster on Tuesday by Adolph Moser

It's Tough to Lose your Balloon by Jarrett J. Krosoczka

Good News, Bad News by Jeff Mack

Some Dogs Do by Jez Alborough

A.N.T. Annoying Nonsense Thoughts: A Guide to Positive Thinking by Sara Parker

Rain Brings Frogs by MaryAnn Cocca-Leffler

The Worst Day of My Life… EVER! By Julia Cook

One of Those Days by Amy Krouse Rosenthal

Bounce Back! A Book About Resilience by Cheri J. Meiners M.Ed.

Everyone is Unique

Calvin Can't Fly by Jennifer Berne

Only One You by Linda Kranz

You be You by Linda Kranz

Rosie's Story by Martine Gogoll

The Sneetches by Dr. Seuss

It's OK to be Different by Todd Parr

Hooray for You: A Celebration of You-Ness by Marianne Richmond

Wink: The Ninja Who Wanted to be Noticed by J.C. Phillipps

Beautiful, Beautiful Hair by Melissa Parkington

Eggbert: The Slightly Cracked Egg by Tom Ross

Back to Front and Upside Down! by Claire Alexander

Video Index to Support Lessons

The pdf (p163_Video Links.pdf) will help you easily open these links. Simply download it at **www.ncyi.org/mindsetmatters** and click on the appropriate link.

Topic	Link	Page	Audience	Length
Background and Overview of Growth Mindset				
Carol Dweck, "Developing a Growth Mindset"	https://www.youtube.com/watch?v=hiiEeMN7vbQ	155	Adult	9:37
Growth Mindset Video	https://www.youtube.com/watch?v=ElVUqv0v1EE	90	Student	2:30
Mindfulness				
"Just Breathe" by Julie Bayer Salzman & Josh Salzman	https://www.youtube.com/watch?v=RVA2N6tX2cg	42,55,57	Student	3:41
Mind in a Jar - Planting Seeds of Mindfulness MOVIE!	https://www.youtube.com/watch?v=QNmMH6tqiMc	42,55,57	Student	1:13
JusTme - My Mindfulness	https://www.youtube.com/watch?v=JUKItN1Z8kw	42	Student	2:38
JusTme Feat. E.E.D.E.E - Mindful or Nah	https://www.youtube.com/watch?v=JBRp2d7-X6k	42	Student	4:15
Sesame Street: Common and Colbie Caillat - "Belly Breathe" with Elmo	https://www.youtube.com/watch?v=_mZbzDOpyIA	42,50,51	Student	2:25
JusTme Im Present	https://www.youtube.com/watch?v=XjIWFqvThBY	42,50,51	Student	3:01
Yoga for Kids: Breathing Warm-Ups	https://www.youtube.com/watch?v=SEC0V8uO048	42	Student	1:17
Mindfulness in Schools: Richard Burnett at TEDxWhitechapel	https://www.youtube.com/watch?v=6mlk6xD_xAQ	43	Adult	19:21
Identify How Your Brain Works				
How To Remember Stuff for Exams (A Sieve-Like Brain)	https://www.youtube.com/watch?v=kQ4Qw0-XnR4	64	Student	1:33
How We Learn - Synapses and Neural Pathways	https://www.youtube.com/watch?v=t4np5wLAhWw	64,68	Student	3:15
Your Brain is Plastic	https://www.youtube.com/watch?v=5KLPxDtMqe8	64	Student	4:07
Structure of a Neuron	https://www.youtube.com/watch?v=Ta_vWUsrjho	64	Student	6:13
How Youth Learn: Ned's GR8 8	https://www.youtube.com/watch?v=p_BskcXTqpM	64	Student	6:12
Brain Jump with Ned the Neuron: Challenges Grow Your Brain	https://www.youtube.com/watch?v=g7FdMi03CzI	27,64,84, 85	Student	1:51
Brain Tricks - This Is How Your Brain Works	https://www.youtube.com/watch?v=JiTz2i4VHFw	64	Student	4:40
How the Brain Works	https://www.youtube.com/watch?v=Y4O_Wkv66b0	64	Student	9:05
The Learning Brain	https://www.youtube.com/watch?v=cgLYkV689s4&t-list=PL411402B45D1OAFCgtindex=12	64,72	Student	7:01
Neuroplasticity	https://www.youtube.com/watch?v=ELpfYCZa87gSkin-dex=628.clist=PLfM-YIRNOOtoPuUcmpGa2avMl6Q0YtbUi	64,73	Student	2:03

© National Center For Youth Issues • www.ncyi.org • 866-318-6294
Please refer to page 2 for duplication information

Not Yet is OK

Title	URL	Pages	Audience	Time
Famous Failures	https://www.youtube.com/watch?v=zLYEClJmnQs	79	Student	2:58
You Can Learn Anything	https://www.youtube.com/watch?v=JC82Il2cjqA	79,84,85	Student	1:30
Jesse Ruben–We Can–OFFICIAL Music Video	https://www.youtube.com/watch?v=59Aj9E5ICn0	79	Student	4:11
Barney Saltzberg's Beautiful Oops, full video	https://www.youtube.com/watch?v=B0A3QhGVyDs	79,89	Student	9:59
Sesame Street: Janelle Monae - Power of Yet	https://www.youtube.com/watch?v=XLeUvZvuvAs	79,90	Student	2:41
Understanding Talent	https://www.youtube.com/watch?v=LfUvchfrcS0	79	Student	2:12

Determination and GRIT

Title	URL	Pages	Audience	Time
Carol Dweck: The Effect of Praise on Mindsets	https://www.youtube.com/watch?v=TTXrV0_3UjY	95	Adult	3:25
TMB Panyee FC short film: Make the Difference	https://www.youtube.com/watch?v=jU4oA3kkAWU	95,108	Student	5:14
How Many Times Should You Try Before Success?	https://www.youtube.com/watch?v=I10vxL0VJO0	96	Student	1:55
Grit: The Key to Your Success at FLVS	https://www.youtube.com/watch?v=uwsZZ2rprqc&feature=youtu.be	96,108	Student	2:22
Amazing Kids of Character: Perseverance (Accessible Preview)	https://www.youtube.com/watch?v=1WXL2peOPG4	96	Student	4:07
Amazing Kids of Character: Portraits of Perseverance	https://www.youtube.com/watch?v=S7vouKO84oI	96,110	Student	1:44
Don't Stop, Don't Give Up!	https://www.youtube.com/watch?v=7uUIOAyQsn4	96,98	Student	1:18
Sesame Street: Bruno Mars: Don't Give Up	https://www.youtube.com/watch?v=pWp6kkz-pnQ	96	Student	1:57
Warhawk Matt Scott in Nike 'No Excuses' Commercial	https://www.youtube.com/watch?v=obdd31Q9PqA	96	Student	1:01
Will Smith Mindset	https://www.youtube.com/watch?v=IJKIgtCpwvg&list=PLfM-YfRNOOtoPuUcmpGa2avM16Q0YtbUi&index=51	96	Student	1:26
The Wall: TV Commercial	http://www.values.com/inspirational-stories-tv-spots/85-The-Wall	103	Student	1:30

Self-Talk

Title	URL	Pages	Audience	Time
Jessica's "Daily Affirmation"	https://www.youtube.com/watch?v=qR3rK0kZFkg	116	Student	0:49
Do or Do not there is no try - Yoda Star Wars: The Empire Strikes Back	https://www.youtube.com/watch?v=eExL1VLkQYk	116	Student	1:00
Teaching Positive Thinking	https://www.youtube.com/watch?v=SQIVsIZIMXI	116	Student	0:49
Positive & Negative Thinking Great Lesson	https://www.youtube.com/watch?v=B-qJ8fu0rrI	116,117	Student	1:59
Power of Positive Thinking	https://www.youtube.com/watch?v=NL1JEn3ahx8	116	Student	1:17
Crabby Little Girl - Clip	https://www.youtube.com/watch?v=TkGLRhHipUk	116	Student	1:41
Finding Nemo - Just Keep Swimming.flv	https://www.youtube.com/watch/?v=hbgD-r-tYzQ	116	Student	0:30
Tiger Tiger Is It True?	www.youtube.com/watch?v=gPfB4CR6fUU&index=1&list=RDgPfB4CR6fUUT	134	Student	6:32

Bonus Videos

Carol Dweck's TED talk	https://www.ted.com/speakers/carol_dweck	25	Adult	10:20
The Power of Believing that You Can Improve	https://www.ted.com/talks/carol_dweck_the_power_of_believing_that_you_can_improve	35	Adult	10:20
Perseverance. The story of Nick Vujicic	https://www.youtube.com/watch?v=gNnVdlvodTQ	108	Student	3:36
The Bouncing Dot Music Video	http://www.fablevisionlearning.com/blog/2014/08/the-dot-song/	122	Student	2:30
Daily Affirmations - Short Positive Affirmations Quotes	https://www.youtube.com/watch?v=rOEqCGtHEwg&feature=share	134	Student	1:52
EGGBERT The Slightly Cracked Egg-EDM310 Kristen Phelps	https://www.youtube.com/watch?v=H-MROaWNZFY	149	Student	1:10
Change your mindset, change the game I Dr. Alia Crum I TEDxTraverseCity	https://www.youtube.com/watch?v=0tqq66zwa7g		Adult	18:20
The Power of Belief - Mindset and Success- Growth mindset vs Fixed mindset	https://www.youtube.com/watch?v=Yn966v5INaI&list=PL411402B45D1OAFC&.index=4		Adult	10:52
Carol Dweck, Growth Mindsets and Motivation	https://www.youtube.com/watch?v=aPNeu07I52w		Adult	8:01
Angela Lee Duckworth: The key to success? Grit	https://www.youtube.com/watch?v=H14bBuluwB8		Adult	6:12

© National Center For Youth Issues • www.ncyi.org • 866-318-6294
Please refer to page 2 for duplication information

References

Dweck, C. S. (2006). *Mindset: The New Psychology of Success.* New York: Random House.

Ricci, M. (2013). *Mindsets in the Classroom: Building a Culture of Success and Student Acheivement in Schools.* Waco, TX: Prufrock Press.

Index for PowerPoints

See page 2 of this book for full copyright and use information.

Download the
PowerPoint file to guide
you through this lesson at:
**www.ncyi.org/
mindsetmatters**

PowerPoint Presentations

If you see this icon, this means the lesson you are reading about has a PowerPoint to guide your lesson. Why recreate the wheel? Use this as a guide for your students and also for you. Visit **www.ncyi.org/ mindsetmatters** and follow the instructions for download.

PowerPoint Video Index

© National Center For Youth Issues • www.ncyi.org • 866-318-6294
Please refer to page 2 for duplication information

Index for Reproducibles

See page 2 of this book for full copyright and use information.

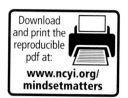

Download and print the reproducible pdf at: www.ncyi.org/ mindsetmatters

Downloadable Reproducibles

The following reproducibles are available for download in pdf form. These pdfs may be printed or used with a SmartBoard. Visit **www.ncyi.org/ mindsetmatters** and follow the instructions for download.

NOTES

© National Center For Youth Issues • www.ncyi.org • 866-318-6294
Please refer to page 2 for duplication information